Becoming the Woman of His Dreams

Sharon Jaynes

HARVEST HOUSE PUBLISHERS

EUGENE, OREGON

Cover by Garborg Design Works, Minneapolis, Minnesota

BECOMING THE WOMAN OF HIS DREAMS
Copyright © 2005 by Sharon Jaynes
Published by Harvest House Publishers
Eugene, Oregon 97402
www.harvesthousepublishers.com

Library of Congress Cataloging-in-Publication Data

Jaynes, Sharon.
  Becoming the woman of his dreams / Sharon Jaynes.
    p. cm.
  Includes bibliographical references.
  ISBN 0-7369-1351-3 (pbk.)
  1. Sex role—Religious aspects—Christianity. 2. Marriage—Religious aspects—Christianity. 3. Man-woman relationships—Religious aspects—Christianity. 4. Christian women—Religious life. I. Title.
BT708.J39 2005
248.8'435—dc22
                                                    2004015768

Printed in the United States of America.

06 07 08 09 10 11 12 13 / VP-CF / 10 9 8 7 6

This book is dedicated to Bruce and Mary Ellen Jaynes,
whose marriage is and will be
a legacy for generations to come.

Acknowledgments

This book would not be possible without the hundreds of men from all walks of life who shared openly and honestly about what they longed for in a wife. Thank you for giving of yourselves by filling out lengthy questionnaires and succumbing to tough interview questions.

A special thanks to so many of my friends who shared part of their lives with me in order to help build strong marriages. I am awed at your willingness to let others see the "not so pretty" parts of your lives. Bonnie Lillie, Linda and Buck Butler, Don and Jona Wright, Gene Vaughan, Jill and Jeremy Tracey, Ted and Beverly Greve...you're the best!

I am also grateful to the incredible staff of Proverbs 31 Ministries for your continued support and encouragement: Lysa TerKeurst, Mary Southerland, Lara LeQuire, Marie Ogram, Barb Spenser, Renee Swope, Micca Campbell, Ginger Plowman, Glynnis Whitwer, Laurie Webster, Shelly Chen, and Van Walton. It is an honor to serve with you in bringing God's peace, perspective, and purpose to today's busy woman.

I am so blessed to once again work with my Harvest House Publishers team: editor Kim Moore, managing editor Betty Fletcher, publicist Teresa Evenson, and editorial managing director Barb Sherrill. A special thanks also to the editorial team of Carolyn McCready, LaRae Weikert, and Terry Glaspey. You are such a joy to work with!

Finally, I am so thankful for my husband, Steve. Thank you for reading and rereading, for sharing your words of wisdom, and for loving me through the process. You are the man of my dreams.

Contents

ONE

An Invitation to Play the Starring Role

"And they lived happily ever after."

Wait a minute. That is supposed to be the end of the story, not the beginning. Well, my friend, I think that has been our problem in marriage all along. To have a great marriage, we must begin with the hoped-for end in mind. Every word we speak, every decision we make, and every action we take will either move us closer to or take us further away from that end.

From the time a little girl first hears fairy tales of the damsel in distress being rescued by the handsome prince, captivated by his pledge of never-ending love, and whisked away on a white steed into the sunset, a dream begins to take shape on the stage of her mind. She hopes and prays that one day *her* prince will come. And then...one day he does! Oh, he may not look like the prince in the storybooks, or even like the one from her childhood imaginings, but he is her prince nonetheless. Will the words "and they lived happily ever after" appear before the final curtain falls? My dear sister, this is not just something we hope for. It is something we work toward. It is the goal, and you, fair lady, have been invited to play the starring role.

Have you ever considered that your husband had similar notions of what his dream wife would be like? As a little boy he probably didn't sit around reading fairy tales about becoming a prince—a warrior, maybe—but not the neat-and-tidy young man who placed his lips upon Snow White's to wake her from a cursed sleep. He most likely skipped the Barbie aisle where Malibu Ken stood with every hair in place on his plastic head and went straight for the G.I. JOEs. Our spouses probably didn't give much thought to what they wanted in a wife until their teen years. However, your husband's vision of a future mate most assuredly began to unfurl when he laid eyes on you.

Remember the courting days? That's when we ladies put our best foot forward—in hopes that the glass slipper will fit. With a smile on our lips and a sparkle in our eyes, we somehow convinced this man that we are what he's been looking for his entire life! The woman of his dreams!

So we buy the beautiful dress, gather with family and friends, and walk down the aisle to say, "I do." Then the organ blasts, and we walk out the door into reality. This is where the glass slipper meets the road. Can we do it? Can we be the woman of our man's dreams? Do we really even want to?

When I married my wonderful husband, Steve, I had no idea what it would take to truly become the woman of his dreams. Oh, he told me that I already was, but I had an inkling there would be more to having a happy marriage than the fact that I loved Steve and Steve loved me. Even on our wedding day, the most beautiful day of my life, I had a suspicion there was more to discovering what it meant to truly become *one*. It didn't take me very long to learn that I was right.

In the Bible, Proverbs 31 describes the wife of noble character. "An excellent wife, who can find? Her worth is far above jewels (Proverbs 31:10 NASB). This gal was smart, skillful, thrifty, industrious, and strong. She had a reverence for God and was a blessed mother, keeper of her home, savvy money manager, faithful friend and mentor, and compassionate servant in the community. She was a powerful force long before Helen Reddy sang "I am woman, hear me roar." And what did her husband think about all her admirable qualities? He praised her saying, "Many women do noble things, but you surpass them all" (Proverbs 31:29).

What would it take for a man to praise his wife at the beginning and end of their lives together and all the days in between? In order to find the answer to that question, I surveyed hundreds of men and had countless interviews. I asked men the following questions:

- How would you describe the woman of your dreams?

- What do you wish your wife understood about you and your longings?

- What does your wife do well that other women could learn from?

- What has been the greatest struggle in your marriage?

- How could your wife help alleviate that problem?

- What is one thing you wish women understood about what a man wants in the woman of his dreams?

As I compiled the interviews and surveys, I noticed seven qualities of the dream wife that kept coming up time and time again, and I have arranged them to fit the acrostic PRAISES. The woman of your man's dreams *prays* for him, *respects* him, *adores* him, *initiates intimate friendship* with him, *safeguards* her marriage, *encourages* him, and *sexually fulfills* him. While each man is as different as the prints on his fingertips, these seven qualities were universal.

I want you to know that I am not coming to you as an expert who knows all there is to know about becoming the woman of my man's dreams. Rather, I am learning right along with you. I discovered so much from the men I talked to throughout this journey. What touched me more than anything was that these men truly love their wives and want to have strong marriages built on a thousand sharings. They were very honest with me, and they felt safe to share what was really on their hearts and minds. However, most did not feel safe enough for me to use their real names. That is a commentary in itself. Because of their honesty, you may see some things you don't like, the hair may bristle on the back of your neck, and you may throw the book down in a huff. But I would encourage you to keep reading if you really want to become the woman of your man's dreams.

Sprinkled throughout the pages are glimpses of various men's hearts as they shared their responses. Who knows? You may even see yourself mirrored in a response or two.

So join me now on a fantastic journey where you are the leading lady with the starring role in the grand drama called marriage, and discover with me the joys of *Becoming the Woman of His Dreams.*

Section One

Prays for Him

TWO

What Does Prayer Have to Do with It?

Okay, ladies, I have a confession to make right from the beginning. Of all the men I surveyed and interviewed, prayer was not at the top of their wish list. However, I know beyond a shadow of a doubt that we cannot become the woman of our man's dreams without it. Prayer must be the foundation for everything we do. And I can promise you this: We can read all the marriage books in print, and even write a few, but without God's empowerment we will fail.

I don't know where you are in your spiritual journey. Perhaps prayer is part of your everyday life and you speak to God as one speaks to a friend. Perhaps prayer is something you do before mealtimes or before you lay your head on the pillow at night. Perhaps you are more comfortable repeating prayers penned by saints who have gone before us. No matter where you are on the continuum between never praying and constant communication with God, this is the place we have to start. If talking to God is a new concept for you, I encourage you to join me in considering how to tap into the only power source that can give you the will, wit, and wisdom to becoming the woman of your man's dreams.

If you've been married for longer than a week, you've probably already noticed that marriage is difficult. We nod and agree when the pastor says, "And the two shall become one," but then we waltz down the aisle and out the door to determine *which one*. Many of us snuff out the candles representing our separate lives and light the unity candle only to begin the process of snuffing each other out.

I remember sitting in front of a mirror on my wedding day, brushing my hair and staring at the reflection of a woman so full of hope and promise. I was overflowing with love for this man of my dreams, who in just a few moments was going to be my husband…forever. Then my musing took a twist. *Doesn't every bride feel this way about her groom on her wedding day? What causes 50 percent of marriages to end in divorce? What could possibly mar this beautiful union?* Staring at myself in the mirror, I made a commitment that when I said the words, "I do," then "I would." I made a promise to God, to my husband, and to myself that I would do everything within my power to make our marriage a success. I quickly learned that "in my power" was not enough; I had to depend on God's power working in and through me to be the wife my husband needs.

Several years ago, when we built our home, I was so anxious to move in that I didn't even wait for the power company to turn the electricity on. The builder told me I needed to wait at least two more weeks, but I had already waited four months longer than he had promised when the project was begun.

"Ma'am," the builder said, "you can't move in this house. The power's not even turned on!"

"Well, how do your men run the construction equipment?" I asked.

"See that little box on the telephone pole?" he pointed out. "The power company puts what's called a saw box on the pole there. It gives us just enough electricity to run our equipment, but certainly not enough to run a house."

"If it's enough for you, then it's enough for me," I countered.

Sensing he was going to lose the battle, he continued. "Okay, here's the deal. You can move in, but you can only turn on a few lights at a time. If you want to take a shower, you have to turn off all the lights and let the water heater warm up for about 30 minutes. Then you have to flip the switch back off when you're done."

Victory was in the air! We moved in. At first it was very exciting, like camping out in a really nice tent. But after a while I grew tired of take-out food and cold showers, and candlelight dinners were no longer romantic. We were thrilled when the power company came a few weeks later and connected our house to the power source. I turned on the lights, took a hot shower, and preheated the oven—all at the same time.

As I sat and watched the men remove the saw box from the telephone pole, I was struck with the similarities of how I live my life at times. God gave me the power of the Holy Spirit the moment I accepted Jesus Christ as my Savior, and He invites me to tap into that power every day. Some days I live on just enough of God's power to get by, and some days I feel as though I'm powered up with all circuits open. The difference comes when I decide to plug into the power source Himself—through prayer.

I never want to live off the saw box again. And I never want to have just enough of God in my life to get by—my marriage depends on it.

Woman of his dreams? Why, some days I've been the woman of his dreams, all right. A nightmare in which I was the star. Then again, some days I have been the woman of his deepest longings and Steve's had a hard time wiping that silly grin off his face. Whether you've spent more time being Cinderella or Cruella De Vil, here's where we start from this day forward—prayer.

> *Describe the woman of my dreams? I'm married to her. She is a very godly woman who loves the Lord. She is patient, forgiving, tender, loving, and puts up with me, warts and all. —Dan*

My wife has a wonderful ability to connect with others and their suffering. What an amazing gift God has given her. —Don

Describe the woman of my dreams? The one I have. She loves Christ, she loves me, and she has been a wonderful mother to our children. —Josh

The woman of my dreams is actually the wife of my prayers. As a teenager who never really dated, I prayed that God would introduce me to a girl to love. He did just that and we've now been married for more than 14 years. She's beautiful both inside and out. She is a loving mother, dedicated worker, and faithful servant in our church. Best of all, I know she loves me and respects me. Looking back, she exceeds everything I ever dreamed of, but she is exactly what I prayed for. —Jim

"A good marriage is not a contract between two persons but a sacred covenant between three."[1]

Our Only Hope

Bonita and her husband were on their way to their honeymoon destination, sitting in first class with two couples who were celebrating their thirty-fifth and fiftieth anniversaries. The flight attendant, a veteran of 25 years of marriage, decided it would be fun for those couples to give the newlyweds marital advice. They basically told them two things: Don't fight over money, and never go to bed angry at one another. As they sat there dreamy-eyed, Bonita remembers thinking, *Piece of cake! Why on earth would I ever fight with this dashing, charming, utterly irresistible man?*

Some of you are smiling already. Why indeed? Fast-forward a few months.

"I distinctly remember the evening I threw that advice to the wind," Bonita explained. "I was sitting at our quaint little kitchen table competently paying the bills. My husband walked in and announced, 'I've been praying about this, and I believe it's time for me to take over the family finances.' I let out a hearty laugh, but upon seeing the seriousness on his face, fear gripped me. Our financial ruin flashed before my eyes, and I blurted out, 'No way!' and proceeded to remind him which one of us was most capable of handling finances. After all, I was the one who entered the marriage debt free and with a savings account."

That night Bonita and her husband broke both rules. They went to bed angry after arguing about money! Over the next few years there were many nights they went to bed angry. But somewhere around the twelfth year of marriage they came to the realization that a lifetime is an awfully long time to feud and, since they were stuck with one another, they might want to work on their communication skills. "When I finally got around to praying and seeking God's Word on the issue (yes, it finally came to that!), I saw that the Lord has a few things to say about conflict in marriage."

"When I finally got around to praying about it..." That's why I'm beginning with prayer. Prayer is not our last resort; it is our only hope—the starting point where we must begin if we even have a chance at becoming the woman of his dreams.

The First Miracle

Shortly after Jesus was baptized, He attended a wedding reception in the town of Cana, in Galilee. Apparently Jesus felt very comfortable at such a party, and I imagine Him laughing, mingling, and having a good time with His friends. Near the end of the festivities, the servants let Mary in on a disaster—they were out of wine. To run out of wine at a Jewish wedding celebration was an embarrassment and disgrace to the hosting family. Mary turned to her Son and said, "They have no more wine" (John

2:3), as if she expected Him to do something about it. I can almost see her raised eyebrow and the mischievous twinkle in her eye.

Jesus said, "Dear woman, why do you involve me? My time has not yet come" (John 2:4).

Mary turned to the servants and said, "Do whatever he tells you" (verse 5). Mary seemed to understand Jesus' power before anyone else.

Jesus told the servants to fill six large 30-gallon stone jars with water. So they filled them "to the brim" (verse 7). Then He told them to draw some out and take it to the master of the banquet.

When they had done so, the master tasted the water that had been turned into wine. He then called the bridegroom aside and said, "Everyone brings out the choice wine first and then the cheaper wine after the guests have had too much to drink; but you have saved the best till now" (verse 10).

I often wonder what would have happened if the servants had filled the pots half full or three-fourths full. I imagine Jesus would have transformed exactly what they put in. Likewise, God will transform just as much of our marriages as we give Him. As for me, I want to "fill it to the brim" and give Him all of my marriage—every bit of it, so that in our winter years, Steve and I will agree…we have saved the best till now.

I truly have the wife of my desires. Once you have met Wendy, you have met the wife of my dreams.
—*Brad*

The woman of my dreams knows who she is and doesn't need anyone to define her but God.
—*Michael*

I would rather my wife spend 15 minutes daily in prayer and Bible study than dusting bookshelves no one sees. —*Bill*

THREE

Then God Created an Intercessor

Do you remember the creation story recorded in Genesis? I never cease to wonder at the marvelous beginning of this book of the Bible I have grown to love: "In the beginning God created the heavens and the earth" (Genesis 1:1). Before the creation of the world, there was nothing. Try to think of nothing. It's hard to do. Then God spoke the world into existence; decorated the sky with the sun, moon, and stars; scattered seed of every kind in the soil; and released flocks of birds into the sky, swarms of insects into the air, and schools of fish into the sea. On the sixth day, God created all the creeping animals, and then He created man in His own image. After each masterpiece was completed, God said, "It is good." The only time God said "It is not good" was when He said, "It isn't good for man to be alone" (Genesis 2:18 TLB).

> But for Adam no suitable helper was found. So the Lord God caused the man to fall into a deep sleep; and while he was sleeping, he took one of man's ribs and closed up the place with flesh. Then the Lord God made a woman from the rib he had taken out of man, and he brought her to the man (Genesis 2:20-22).

The New American Standard Bible says God "fashioned" Eve. He took extra special care when He created you. As a matter of fact, woman was God's grand finale!

Up to this point in the Genesis recording of creation, Adam had remained silent. However, when he saw the fair Eve, I imagine he said, "Whoa! Now this is good!" We don't know for sure, but we do know that his first recorded words after laying eyes on God's magnificent gift to him were: "This is now bone of my bones and flesh of my flesh; she shall be called 'woman,' for she was taken out of man" (Genesis 2:23). Eve was created to complete man like two pieces of a puzzle fitting together. The word "complete" means "to fill up; that which is required to supply a deficiency; one or two mutually completing parts."

Let's look at Genesis 2:18 from several different translations of the Bible:

> And the Lord God said, "It isn't good for man to be alone. I will make a companion for him, a helper suited to his needs" (TLB).

> Now the Lord God said, It is not good (sufficient, satisfactory) that the man should be alone; I will make him a helper meet (suitable, adapted, complementary) for him (AMP).

> The LORD God said, "It is not good for the man to be alone. I will make a helper suitable for him" (NIV).

> Then the LORD God said, "It is not good that the man should be alone; I will make him a helper fit for him" (RSV).

> And the LORD God said, It is not good that the man should be alone; I will make him a help meet for him (KJV).

While each translation of the Bible uses a different combination of words, they each contain the word "helper." The man was not better than the woman (he was lacking without her). The woman was not better than the man (she was lacking without him). Paul wrote, "However, in the Lord, neither is woman independent of man, nor is man independent of woman" (1 Corinthians 11:11 NASB). We were designed to depend on and complement each other. The Greek word for "helper" can also be translated "partner." "Just as the rib is found at the side of the man and is attached to him, even so the good wife, the rib of her husband, stands at his side to be his helper-counterpart, and her soul is bound up with his."[2]

While some may bristle at the thought of being called a mere "helper," we need only to look at the pages of Scripture to see that a helper holds a place of great honor. The word for "helper" that is used for woman (*ezer*) is derived from the Hebrew word used of God and the Holy Spirit (*azar*).[2] Both mean "helper"—one who comes alongside to aid or assist. King David wrote, "O LORD, be my helper" (Psalm 30:10 NASB). "The LORD is with me; he is my helper" (Psalm 118:7). Moses said of God, "My father's God was my helper; he saved me from the sword of the Pharaoh" (Exodus 18:4). In the New Testament, Jesus told the disciples that when He ascended to heaven, His Father would send them another Helper, the Holy Spirit (John 14:16 NASB). When we consider that the same title is used for both God and woman, we can see "helper" as a position of honor.

Interestingly, studies of the prison population show that a large majority of inmates are single men. "It isn't good for man to be alone." My husband told me about a study that showed that men drove more safely when their wives were in the car, and had fewer wrecks and speeding tickets. "It isn't good for man to be alone." We are called to come alongside and help.

A Prayer Warrior

Of all the roles and responsibilities God has given us as wives, the position of a prayer warrior or intercessor is perhaps the greatest of all. An intercessor is a person who intervenes or prays for another person. It was derived from the Greek word *enteuxis*, which means to go before a king with a petition or plea on behalf of someone else.[3] In essence, it means the same thing today. We go before the King of Kings with a petition or plea on our husband's behalf. What we accomplish on our knees in the invisible realm will ultimately affect the strength of our marriage in the visible realm. There is no other person who is more called or more qualified to pray for your man than you.

In the Bible, God describes the marriage of a man and a woman as a visual example of the spiritual union between Jesus Christ and the church (all Christians). Believers are called "the bride" of Christ (Revelation 19:7). We are walking, talking earthly examples of the heavenly relationship between God's Son and those who believe on His name. God instructs men, "Love your wives just as Christ also loved the church and gave Himself up for her" (Ephesians 5:25 NASB).

There is someone who wants to destroy that living example, and his name is Satan. Jesus said, "The thief [Satan] comes only to steal and kill and destroy" (John 10:10). He desires to destroy the God-ordained-and-designed institution of marriage. He began with Adam and Eve in the Garden of Eden and continues his destructive tactics even today. Satan is not very creative, but he's very effective, and he uses the same temptations and tactics now that he used in the first marriage on earth. He has proclaimed an all-out assault on the family, and he begins at the top—with the husband and wife.

So many times we fail to see the real enemy in our marital struggles. Paul explains: "For our struggle is not against flesh and blood, but against the rulers, against the authorities, against the powers of this dark world and against the spiritual forces of evil in the heavenly realms" (Ephesians 6:12). When I am having a conflict with my husband, I need to stop, take a deep breath, and think, *Who is the real enemy here?* There is a spiritual battle raging all around us that we can't even see, but it is a greater reality than what our five senses detect. It is a battle not to be feared but to be recognized and fought in the only place where it can be won—in prayer.

Perhaps one of the clearest examples of this spiritual battle is recorded in 2 Kings 6. The king of Aram was furious with the prophet Elisha because he continued to reveal his battle plans to the king of Israel. During the night the king of Aram sent horses and chariots and a strong force to surround the city where Elisha was stationed. When the sun peeked over the horizon, Elisha's servant pulled back the curtain and stood in horror at their certain doom.

"Oh, my lord, what shall we do?" the servant asked.

"Don't be afraid," Elisha calmly replied. "Those who are with us are more than those who are with them."

Elisha prayed, "O LORD, open his eyes so he may see." Then the LORD opened the servant's eyes, and he looked and saw the hills full of horses and chariots of fire all around Elisha" (2 Kings 6:8-17).

Elisha knew that God's warring angels were there to protect them, defend them, and fight the battle for them. While most likely we will never have the privilege of having the curtain that separates the seen from the unseen parted as Elisha's servant did, we can be sure that God has His angels in place to minister to us in mighty ways (Hebrews 1:14). There is a battle raging for our marriage, our husband, and our own loyalties. But just as Elisha encouraged his servant, "Those who are with us are more than those who are with them," we also have the Lord on our side!

In Ephesians 6:13-17, Paul describes the armor God provides for each of us to fight those spiritual battles. The helmet of salvation protects our head, the breastplate of righteousness protects our heart and vital organs, the peace of God protects our feet, the belt of God's truth holds it all together, and the shield of faith (holding up what we know to be true) blocks the fiery darts of the devil. All the pieces of the armor are for defense except for one—the sword of the Spirit, which is the Word of God. With the truth of God's Word, we fight the lies of the enemy.

When Jesus was tempted by Satan in the desert after fasting for 40 days, He had only one weapon of defense, and it was the same weapon that is available to you and me. He used Scripture to fight the enemy. "It is written…it is written…it is written," Jesus said. Satan couldn't stand up under that kind of attack, so he fled. "Resist the devil, and he will flee from you," James tells us (James 4:7). Satan can't stand the Word of God, and he can't stand up to the Word of God.

> For though we live in the world, we do not wage war as the world does. The weapons we fight with are not the weapons of the world. On the contrary, they have divine power to demolish strongholds. We demolish arguments and every pretension that sets itself up against the knowledge of God, and we take captive every thought to make it obedient to Christ (2 Corinthians 10:3-5).

Notice in Ephesians that there is only one weapon of offense, but in 2 Corinthians 10:3-5 above we see the word "weapons" (plural). When prayer and the Word of God are combined, we will have a dynamic prayer life that will demolish, destroy, and divert the devil's attacks. Satan loves it when we're busy, but he hates it when we pray. He would much rather we get all worried about our problems and try to work them out on our own, but when we begin to pray, Satan begins to wring his hands.

Yes, there is an enemy who wants to destroy, but there is also a Redeemer who wants us to have an abundant, fulfilling, and lifelong marriage. Jesus said, "I came that they may have and enjoy life, and have it in abundance (to the full, till it overflows)" (John 10:10 AMP). No wonder His first miracle was at a party—a wedding celebration at that!

One of the greatest benefits of prayer is that we grow in our intimacy with God. Yes, He wants to heal our marriages, but He also wants us to know Jehovah-rapha, the One who heals. Yes, He wants to provide for our needs, but He wants us to have a relationship with Jehovah-jireh, the God who provides. Yes, He wants us to have a marriage based on love, but he also wants us to know the One who is love.

Praying for your husband is synonymous with praying for yourself. When we are married, we are joined together as one flesh. Therefore, praying for your man is like praying for the other half of your very being.

Prayer is powerful. God's Word is powerful. And when we light the gunpowder of God's Word with the fire of our prayers, we have a powerful tool. When we pray God's Word, we begin to take every thought captive that doesn't line up with the truth. In a sense, we are renewing our minds or changing the way we think (Romans 12:2). And changing the way we think or believe is the first step to changing the way we act.

In the appendix I have included a guide for praying Scripture for your husband from head to toe. You may want to pray for one part of his body per day, or cover him from head to toe on a daily basis.

> *The woman of my dreams believes in me and prays for me to succeed.* —Bob

> *My wife is the woman of my dreams. She prioritizes caring for our family, which is easy for her because she enjoys and values being a wife and mother. The way she manages our home makes each person feel like the most important person in the world. She is great at homemaking skills and saving money. She takes great care of herself physically. She prods me to work less and spend more time doing stuff I like, which makes me feel as though she really*

wants me to be happy. She maintains a fun, youthful excitement about simple pleasures like walks in the country, trips to the beach, and visits to the local farms to buy fresh vegetables. She doesn't want a fancy house or car but appreciates a simple lifestyle, which relieves me of the pressure to make more money than I do. —Gene

The woman of my dreams is the woman I married 45 years ago. We've certainly had our struggles… my alcohol abuse, controlling temper, etc., but God put us together and I praise Him for helping us grow in His Word. —James

One of my biggest struggles has been keeping my priorities straight. God—family—job is the prescription, but I always reversed the order. My wife used patience and perseverance to help me come around as we both changed and grew to realize that the only person we can change is ourselves. —Bill

One of my biggest struggles is with lust. My wife could help me by praying for me and allowing me to be honest with her about my need for physical intimacy and closeness. —Joe

Joan and I were 17 and 19 when we got married. She was ready, but I was not. She stuck with me, even through alcoholism (which I gave up when I was 30). With all the vision and bravado of a young man, I saw she could be my wife no matter how far or how low life took me. Forty years have proved that she is a gem beyond compare. —Bart

Praying vs. Nagging

There are some verses in the Bible that I wish God had just left out. Here are a few of them:

- A quarrelsome wife is like a constant dripping (Proverbs 19:13).

- A quarrelsome wife is like a constant dripping on a rainy day; restraining her is like restraining the wind or grasping oil with the hand (Proverbs 27:15-16).

- Better to live in a desert than with a quarrelsome and ill-tempered wife (Proverbs 21:19).

- Better to live on a corner of the roof than share a house with a quarrelsome wife (Proverbs 25:24).

Okay, that's about all I can take right now. One thing that men repeatedly mentioned in the surveys and interviews was their aversion to a wife's nagging. Drip, drip, drip. My dictionary defines nagging as *to scold or find fault with repeatedly, to cause annoyance by scolding or repetition.* Interestingly, a nag is also an *inferior or aged horse.* The best remedy to cure ourselves from being a nagging wife is to become a praying wife. Jesus invites us to stop nagging our husbands and begin nagging God!

> Then he said to them, "Suppose one of you has a friend, and he goes to him at midnight and says, 'Friend, lend me three loaves of bread, because a friend of mine on a journey has come to me, and I have nothing to set before him.' Then the one inside answers, 'Don't bother me. The door is already locked, and my children are with me in bed. I can't get up and give you anything.' I tell you, though he will not get up and give him the bread because he is his friend, yet because of the man's boldness he will get up and give him as much as he

needs. So I say to you: Ask and it will be given to you; seek and you will find; knock and the door will be opened to you. For everyone who asks receives; he who seeks finds; and to him who knocks, the door will be opened" (Luke 11:5-9).

In the above passage of Scripture, the words for "ask," "seek," and "knock" are present participle verbs. This means that a more literal translation would read: "Ask and keep on asking, seek and keep on seeking, knock and keep on knocking." God invites us to be persistent in our prayers for our husbands. We can give our worries and cares to Him and leave it up to Him to do the rest. In both the Old and New Testaments of the Bible, God encourages us to give our worries to Him. "Cast your cares on the LORD and he will sustain you" (Psalm 55:22). "Cast all your anxiety on him because he cares for you" (1 Peter 5:7). Remember, you don't want to be your husband's mother…you want to be the wife of his dreams.

Something else we must consider is God's timetable. God says that your husband is His workmanship—not yours. God is the artist on the canvas of your husband's life. When we grab the brush away from God, we are interfering with His work of art. Too many times we strive to conform our husbands into our image of the perfect mate, sabotaging God's efforts to conform him into His image of the perfect man—Jesus Christ.

Linda wanted desperately for her husband to come to know Christ as his Savior. She dreaded going to church and sitting in the pew alone. It seemed people walked in the church like Noah's animals…two by two. But Linda sat and worshiped by herself.

Linda's husband had a name that suited his personality— Buck. Buck was a high school teacher and football coach who, at age 12, had informed his Episcopalian mother that he was no longer going to church. "I'm simply not interested and I'm not going to go," he resolved. But then he fell in love with Linda, a redheaded and determined Baptist.

After they were married, Linda continued to attend church, each time asking Buck if he'd like to come along. The answer was always the same, "No." Linda began to pray for Buck and asked her parents and their friends to join her. (What she didn't know was the little band of prayer warriors had been praying all along.) Linda never nagged Buck about his decision not to attend church or not to participate in any "religious" activities. She simply prayed and continued to invite him to come with her.

After about a year, Buck surprised Linda and said he'd like to tag along to a couple's Bible study. While there he observed how this group of friends loved each other and, amazingly, loved him. Never once did he feel out of place or unaccepted. After attending four of the weekly meetings, as the group ended in prayer, Buck surprised them all.

"Lord," he prayed, "I come to You tonight admitting that I'm a sinner. I know that I can't make it without You, and I'm asking now if You will be my Redeemer and come into my life. I accept You as my Lord and Savior."

The group was shocked. The angels were jumping with joy. Linda was beside herself with tears streaming down her cheeks. *Did that just happen?* she wondered.

Buck later told me, "I know it was Linda's prayers and the prayers of her parents that softened my heart. It was so uncharacteristic of me to even agree to go to a Bible study. The old Buck would have never stepped foot in such a place. But God began a work in my heart through my wife's prayers. She never nagged me or pushed me. If she had, I would have planted my feet and strengthened my resolve to stay away from spiritual things. She simply loved me, prayed for me, and invited me to join her. Once I went to the Bible study, I met incredible people who had a peace and joy that I wanted in my own life."

Linda and Buck have been married for 27 years.

Augustine advised, "Do what you can do, and pray for what you cannot do." Changing our husbands falls into the category of "what you cannot do." You do the praying and let God do the changing.

Praying for Ourselves

I have a question. Why do we want to become the woman of his dreams? Is it so we can get what we want in the long run? Is it so that when he sees how irresistible we are he'll magically become the man of our dreams and meet our every need? Is it perhaps so we can gain control and wrap him around our little finger?

These are good questions. But becoming the wife of his dreams won't happen until we decide we would rather win his heart than win the battle, do right than be right, give more than get more, and wrap our arms around him instead of wrap him around our little finger. Becoming the woman of his dreams involves sacrifice. It involves praying constantly for him, respecting him as a man and a leader, adoring him as the one who makes your heart skip a beat, initiating intimate friendship with him through creating commonalities, safeguarding your marriage by putting him second to no other earthly relationship, encouraging him in his pursuits and dreams, and sexually fulfilling him. Many times this means denying ourselves and putting our man's needs above our own.

Did you realize we can pray for our husbands with wrong motives? James said, "When you ask, you do not receive, because you ask with wrong motives, that you may spend what you get on your pleasures" (James 4:3). Ouch! Does that mean I can't pray that Steve will change his mind about that new den sofa I want? Hmm. The goal for praying for our husbands is not to get them to do what *we* want, but for them to do what *God* wants.

Hollywood tells us that we will be happy when we "find the right person." However, I have discovered that a successful marriage occurs when we *become* the right person. "For years I prayed that God would change my husband," Denise told me. "Our marriage went from bad to worse, and we ended up separated and headed for divorce. Then I began to read about what it meant to be a godly wife. In the world's eyes I was doing a pretty good job. In God's eyes I was missing the mark. So I began to pray—this time for my own heart. God gave me the answer to my prayer to change my husband…He changed me."

How do we begin to pray for ourselves to become the woman of our man's dreams? A good place to start is by taking a look at the Bible's definition of love found in 1 Corinthians 13. Among other versions, here's a paraphrase you might want to consider…

If I teach Bible study classes, volunteer for women's ministry, and sing in the choir, but do not love my husband, I am only a resounding gong or a clanging cymbal. If I have a college degree, high-paying job, and successful career, but do not love my husband, I am emotionally and spiritually bankrupt. If I have faith that can move mountains, am quick to pray for those in need, and even have half the Bible memorized, but do not love my husband, I am disobedient and do not please God. If I keep a spotless house, maintain a well-manicured lawn, and prepare nutritionally balanced meals, but do not love my husband, it is all for naught. Hired hands can do as much.

Lord, help me to be patient. Help me to be kind. I pray that I will not envy others who have seemingly happier marriages and husbands who are more helpful around the house or thoughtful or romantic. I pray that I will never try to lift myself up by putting my husband down. Lord, I pray that I will not be a proud woman who refuses to listen to her husband, who always has to have the last word, who always thinks her way is best. I pray that I will not be rude to my husband with curt comments, disregard his needs, or be ungrateful for all he does and is, but treat him with respect and honor that the king of a castle deserves.

I pray that I will not be self-serving, always thinking about what is best for me, but thinking of what would be best for my husband. I pray that I will not be angered easily, not hold a grudge, not keep a record of wrongs, not plan ways to retaliate, and not use my tongue as a weapon to cause pain. I pray that I will not rejoice and say "I told you so" when things don't work out the way my husband hoped.

Lord, above all, I pray that my husband will see me as his chief cheerleader who desires to rejoice with him in his victories, both big and small. That he will see me as one who longs to protect our marriage and our love. Help me to create a warm and loving environment in which he feels safe, wanted, and revered. I pray that You will give me endurance when things get tough. Help the word "divorce" to never enter my mind or cross my lips as an option. Lord, I know that love never fails and that You never fail. Fill me with Your Holy Spirit to give me the endurance to stand up under trials and love my husband as You would have me love him—till death do us part.

In Jesus' name, amen.

FOUR

Prayer Changes People

I am always stunned when I hear someone say, "Well, I guess the only thing left to do is pray." My goodness, I've even been shocked to hear those words come out of my own mouth. Prayer should never be seen as a last resort but as a first line of defense. No matter what condition your marriage is in today, prayer will make it better. God can make a bad marriage good and a good marriage great. God's answers to prayer healed the sick, fed the hungry, stopped the rain, kept the earth from revolving on its axis for an hour, divided the Red Sea, poured forth water from a rock, opened wombs, confused enemies, unlocked jail doors, made leprous skin reform, caused the lame to dance, gave courage to the fearful, and raised the dead. Jesus said, "If you have faith as small as a mustard seed, you can say to this mountain 'Move from here to there' and it will move. Nothing will be impossible for you" (Matthew 17:20).

Have you noticed that it's hard to stay mad at someone when you're praying for them? Somehow walking into the throne room of God with a pack of anger and resentment strapped on your back doesn't feel comfortable. It's like those images in the *Highlights* magazines…"What's wrong with this picture?"

I've noticed that when I'm angry at my husband but begin to pray for him (and I'm not talking God-help-him-when-I-get-a-hold-of-him prayers), God begins to soften my heart. The Bible says that God is love, and I have found that it is difficult to be in Love's very presence and remain angry. Oh, you *can* stay mad, but it takes a lot of effort.

Sometimes it is hard to pray for our husbands when we're mad at them. But God tells us to "pray for our enemies." How much more should we pray for our God-given, lifelong mate!

I know there are many of you who are holding this book in your hands and hurt in your hearts. You may be wondering, *How did my marriage drift so far from where I hoped it would be? How did my marriage get to this state of desperation, mediocrity, frigidity, mutual tolerance, and coexistence? Is it too late for me? Is it too late for us?*

Friend, the answer is no—it is not too late. I have good news for you. God's specialty is resurrection. He excels at bringing life from death. In the Old Testament, there was a couple you may have heard of, Abraham and Sarah. God promised Abraham he would have descendants more numerous than the stars in the sky. But there was one problem: His wife Sarah was infertile. Several times God reminded Abraham of his promised progeny, but Sarah's birthdays continued to roll by with no hope of a child. Then, when Abraham was 99 years old and Sarah was 89, the Lord again visited Abraham and reiterated His promise to make Abraham's descendants more numerous than the stars in the sky.

"I will surely return to you about this time next year and Sarah your wife will have a son" (Genesis 18:12). This was too much for Sarah. When she heard the prediction of a baby within the year, she laughed. God heard the snicker and asked, "Is anything too hard for the Lord?" (verse 14).

The following year, the joke was on her. She had a baby boy and named him Isaac, which means "laughter."

Nothing is too hard for God, my friend. Absolutely nothing. He raised Lazarus, the widow from Nain's son, and Jesus Christ from the dead. In Ezekiel 37:1-10, we read how He even took a bunch of old dried-up bones and brought them back to life. "I will make breath enter you, and you will come to life. I will attach tendons to you and make flesh come upon you and cover you with skin; I will put breath in you, and you will come to life. Then you will know that I am the LORD" (Ezekiel 37:5-6). God took that valley of dry bones and raised up a vast army. Nothing, absolutely nothing, is impossible for God.

Jesus said, "All things are possible to him [or her] who believes" (Mark 9:23 NASB). A baby is born to a dried-up womb, fingers and toes materialize on a leper's hands and feet, sight is given to a man blind from birth, and a son is raised right in the middle of his own funeral procession. Now, tell me, is there anything in your life too hard for a God like this?

Where It All Begins

I have so many stories of how prayer has changed men's lives, but I have chosen to tell you about a man named Allan. Allan was raised by a single mother with five other siblings in eastern North Carolina. His father died when he was five years old, and his country mother had the daunting task of raising her six children during the final years of the Great Depression.

As a young man, Allan worked at a small-town lumber company by driving a delivery truck. He graduated from high school at 17, became a soldier in the Korean War at 18, became a husband at 19, and became a father at 20. Over the next 30 years, Allan moved from driving a delivery truck to managing a prosperous building supply company. He and his wife, Louise, had another child when he was 25 and then another when he was 28.

Financially, life was moving along quite well for Allan and Louise; however, there was a secret in their household very few knew. Allan had a severe drinking problem. He didn't drink every day, but when he did, the alcohol consumed him and transformed him into a vicious man. Most of the time his violent outbursts were aimed at his wife. Unfortunately, his children watched in terror as he shattered furniture, hit their mother with his fist, and cut the family to pieces with harsh and cruel words.

Alcohol was not the only vice in Allan's life. While it was never discussed in their home, his bouts with gambling, pornography, and other women were the unspoken reality.

But something amazing happened as Allan approached 40. His 14-year-old daughter befriended a woman in her neighborhood who introduced her to Jesus Christ. His teenage daughter fell in love with Jesus. He wasn't quite sure what to think about her newfound faith. "It's a phase," he told her. "I'm sure it will pass. Just don't go overboard."

Through the years Louise had become a very bitter woman. As you can imagine, living with a man with such a reputation was enough to destroy any woman, but for some reason, she never left him. Louise became intrigued with her daughter's faith but had a difficult time trusting in a God who had allowed such heartache in her life. Their daughter began to pray for both parents to come to know Christ as their Savior, and after two years it seemed her mom's cold heart was beginning to melt.

God did answer the young girl's prayer, and her mom accepted Jesus as her personal Lord and Savior. This is where I want to bring you, dear friends. Yes, God intervened in a young girl's life. Yes, He saved her mother as well. But could God get ahold of Allan's heart? A drinker, carouser, womanizer, gambler, just to name a few of his more colorful attributes? Could God do that?

Louise and her daughter began to pray that God would soften Allan's hardened heart. For years they prayed, and little by little they witnessed God chisel away at his tough exterior.

"I'll stop drinkin'," Allan said one night, "but I cannot become a Christian. I've done some terrible things in my life, and I don't think God could ever forgive me. I could never be good enough."

"Oh, Daddy," the young girl replied, "God will forgive you just as soon as you ask. Besides, we can never be good enough. If we could, Jesus wouldn't have had to die for our sins on the cross."

As God began to soften Allan's heart, he did indeed stop drinking—cold turkey. That in itself was a miracle. But there was still a volcano of anger that always rumbled just below the surface, and Louise never knew when that anger would erupt and spew the lava of hatred and bitterness in their lives. She continued to pray for her husband and believed God for a miracle.

Three years after Louise had given her life to the Lord and begun her journey of praying for her husband, Allan experienced a symphony of twists and turns that only God could have orchestrated. He resigned from the company where he had served as manager to begin his own building supply business with four other investors. However, his previous employer sued him and held him to a restrictive covenant contract that forbade him from working within a 60-mile radius in a company that would be a competitor. He was facing court, exposure for God only knew what, and ruination in the small town in which he lived. Buckling under the pressure, Allan was heading towards a nervous breakdown and total loss of control.

Now God had him just where He wanted him. Allan hit rock bottom, and the only place to go was to reach up. Louise had gone to a business meeting in Pennsylvania and Allan desperately needed to be with her. He drove 500 miles, but he didn't go to her hotel. Instead, he drove to a church and begged for someone to pray for him.

"What denomination are you?" the receptionist asked.

"I don't know. I guess I'd say Baptist," he replied.

"Here," she said as she jotted down directions on a piece of paper. "Our pastor isn't in today, but I happen to know that Clyde Barnes, the pastor of the Baptist church down the street, is out doing some construction on their new church building. Why don't you drive on over and find him? I bet he can help."

So Allan hopped back in his car and drove to a church in the country where he found a man with a hammer in his hand and Jesus in his heart.

"What can I do for you?" the pastor asked.

"I need you to pray for me," Allan explained with tears running down his weathered face.

"Let's sit down here on this log while you tell me what's going on."

For several hours Allan sat on a log with a fellow builder and told him all he had ever done. Amazingly, the very things Allan had felt God could never forgive him of, this pastor had done as well. After five years of a young girl's prayers for her daddy and three years of a wife's prayers for her husband, Allan knelt in the woods, asked God to forgive him of all his sins, and he received Jesus Christ as his personal Lord and Savior. That day, Allan became a new creation in Christ—and it all began with prayer.

Later he explained. "I told that man all I had ever done and he said he had done the same things. I figured that if God could forgive him, and even let him be a preacher, then He could forgive me too."

Amazing grace, how sweet the sound.

For me, this is more than a sweet story. It is a miraculous memory. Allan was my daddy.

Friends, I have seen the power of prayer change lives. It all began right there in my own home as a teenage girl. You know, my mean ol' dad became one of the sweetest men I've ever known. He died from Alzheimer's disease at the age of 66, and his caretakers were always amazed at the smile on his face and the sweetness of his heart.

Do you want to become the wife of your husband's dreams? It all begins with prayer.

Section Two

Respects Him

FIVE

The One Thing
He Can't Do Without

I've been shut up, shut down, shot down, ridiculed, disregarded, overlooked, overbooked, and overwhelmed…I know I was made for a reason. I know that, in God's eyes, I count. So, I simply want to find someone who believes in me.

These are not the lyrics from the latest country song; they are the lamentations from one of my survey respondents. It seems Aretha Franklin isn't the only one who wants a little r-e-s-p-e-c-t these days. One area that rated very high in my survey for men describing the wife of their dreams was RESPECT. My dictionary defines respect as *the special esteem or consideration in which one holds another person or thing, the state or quality of being esteemed, to feel or show consideration to.* It's the one thing a happy husband can't do without.

This is what some of the men in my survey had to say about respect.

> *My greatest struggle has been to have my wife remember that her role is to trust God's leading through me and not regard me as an enemy. I wish she respected me as the spiritual head of the home, even though she may think she is more qualified to*

lead herself. God is sovereign despite my mistakes. My decisions for us do not take God by surprise. —Jared

The woman of my dreams shows respect when no one else is around. —Bill

My wife shows great respect by not taking any disagreements we have beyond us. She doesn't bring her mom or friends in on it. She protects our marriage in this way. —Justin

The wife of my dreams is one that shows her love for her husband through respect and honor, building him up and supporting him as the world seeks to grind him down. —Brian

What is one thing I wish women understood about what a man wants in the woman of his dreams? I wish that women understood how much a man needs a woman to respect him. It is imperative for a woman to value her husband's leadership, his emotions, his desires, his faith, and his intelligence. The importance for a woman to respect her husband's spiritual, financial, and emotional leadership is essential for a strong relationship. I see many women criticize their husbands and try to be the dominant half of the marriage, while the husband feels stupid, belittled, and subservient, driving a deep wedge between them that is difficult to heal. —Nathan

The Danger of Disrespect

Don was 27 years old when Jona first met him on a spring church beach retreat. She immediately knew he was exactly what she had always dreamed of in a husband. Don had a strong faith in God, a good job, a college degree, drive, and dreams for the future. He was physically fit, witty, adventurous, sexy, and just plain gorgeous. On top of that, he was constantly surrounded by women at the retreat who were vying for his attention.

When they returned home, Jona could hardly believe her good fortune when Don asked her to dinner. Don and Jona dated only three months before he asked her to marry him, and on March 30, 1985, before the next spring beach retreat, they were husband and wife.

Their first year of marriage was a blissful blur of candlelight dinners, spontaneous lovemaking, and endless conversation. The icing on the one-year anniversary cake was the purchase of their first home. By their second anniversary, Don had quit his job to start his own business. Life was clicking along at a steady pace toward acquiring the American Dream. By their fourth anniversary, Jona had their first child and joined the ranks of stay-at-home moms. But, after 24 months of Don's new business venture, the couple faced a second mortgage, a dwindling bank account, and a looming cloud of debt. Jona was forced to go back to work, and seeds of discontentment, disrespect, and disenchantment began to take root.

"I was so mad at Don for the mistakes I felt he had made," Jona explained. "Deep down I wanted him to be God and fulfill all my needs. He made a poor God. When my mother died in 1993, I sank into clinical depression. I spent most of my time at home in bed. And even though I had two children by this time, I withdrew from being a mom as well as being a wife. I then began to eat...and eat. I went from 140 pounds to 240 pounds.

"Don and I had the perfect engagement, a beautiful wedding, and a fantasy honeymoon. But when the obstacles came along, I wasn't prepared to maneuver over, around, or through them. I thought, *This is not the way the story goes. What happened to the fairy tale?*

"Don changed jobs about every other year. And even though he always provided for our needs, it drove me crazy that he couldn't stay put.

"I remember one day Don said, 'Why are you eating and gaining all this weight?' I shot back, 'I'm doing this because I don't want you to touch me. Besides, I can lose the weight if I want to, but you'll always be a loser.' Little by little, word by word, angry look by angry look, rejection by rejection, I began the process of destroying my husband. Comments like 'You're so stupid,' 'Duh,' and 'Can't you do anything right?' were constantly spewing from my mouth. I was in pain and I wanted Don to be in pain too. One day I made a list of all Don's faults. He found the list, but I didn't even care."

Jona always thought that because Don was a Christian, he would never leave her. However, there came a point where he could not take the emotional turmoil any longer. On May 6, 2001, Don left the home that had become his prison cell and whipping post. Jona had destroyed her marriage and her man. On January 31, 2003, the divorce was final.

"A couple of months after our divorce, I woke up to God's still small voice," Jona explained. "He seemed to say, 'Is this what you wanted? Did you want a divorce? Do you want Don to marry another woman and have your children torn between spending time in two different households? Do you want to be alone? Were you the wife I called you to be?' Oh, God," Jona cried, "what have I done?"

God's Command

In the Bible, Paul wrote to both men and women about their various roles in marriage. "Each one of you [men] also must love his wife as he loves himself, and the wife must respect her husband" (Ephesians 5:33). Now that doesn't mean that husbands don't need to respect their wives or wives don't need to love their husbands. I believe Paul was summing up what was paramount for both men and women. We want to be loved and cherished just as our husbands want to be honored and respected.

Another reason I believe that Paul admonishes wives to respect their husbands is because he knew that after years of mistakes, poor choices, wrong decisions, and smelly socks, respect may not come naturally for a wife. It may well take an act of obedience empowered by the Holy Spirit within.

But how do you respect someone who vegetates in front of the TV all the time? How do you respect someone who sits around waiting for the right job to come along when you're working yourself to death trying to keep food on the table? (You may need to stop and quietly put that responsibility back where it belongs.) How do you respect someone who apparently has no respect for himself? It may seem impossible, but as the angel asked Abraham, "Is anything too hard for the LORD?" (Genesis 18:14). The same God who caused the walls of Jericho to fall with a shout and who kept Shadrach, Meshach, and Abednego from even having a hint of smoke as they exited the fiery furnace—that same God can give you the power to respect your husband. It all goes back to Section One...becoming the wife of his dreams begins with prayer. There is "incomparably great power" available to those who believe (Ephesians 1:19).

In the Bible, *power* always follows *obedience*. As soon as the high priests crossing the Jordan placed their feet in the water, the river stopped flowing from upstream (Joshua 3:15-16). As soon as the rotting lepers turned toward Jerusalem to tell the priests they were healed, their skin began to heal (Luke 17:14). As soon as Naaman dipped into the river seven times as the prophet Elisha had commanded, his leprosy began to disappear (2 Kings 5:14). The miracle didn't come before they obeyed, but after they obeyed. Do you want to see a miracle unfold before your eyes like a multi-petaled rose unfurling? Obey God.

An amazing thing happens when we begin to show respect to our husbands. They begin to act respectable. Let's go back to Paul's letter to the Ephesians. I love how the Amplified Version expounds on Ephesians 5:33. "Let the wife see that she respects and reverences her husband [that she notices him, regards him, honors him, prefers him, venerates, and esteems him; and that she defers to him, praises him, and love and admires him exceedingly]." What a power-packed verse!

Karol Ladd, author of *The Power of a Positive Wife*, said, "Respect is wrapped up in the beautiful paper of kind and gentle words and tied with the enormous ribbons of a loving spirit."[1] It is one of the most beautiful gifts a wife can give.

In the following chapters we'll look at three elements of respect: the gift of leadership, the gift of a contented wife, and the gift of an attractive wife.

> *The one thing I wish my wife understood about me is my need for respect, honor, and admiration.* —*Bart*

> *When a man doesn't feel admired and respected by his wife, he feels emasculated and becomes angry inside.* —*Chad*

> *The woman of a man's dreams saves disagreements for the privacy of their own home. She expresses her viewpoints, but allows him to make decisions without being second-guessed or doubted. She supports him, whether right or wrong, especially in public.* —*Craig*

SIX

Two Heads Are Not Always Better Than One

Oh, boy. You knew I'd get around to this eventually, so let's go ahead and get it all out on the table. The woman of his dreams is one who submits to his leadership and authority in the home and in the marriage relationship. There. I said it.

Let me share a visual example of the problem of submission (or, rather, the lack thereof) from my book *Becoming a Woman Who Listens to God*.

Several years ago, Steve and I decided to take ballroom dance classes. I had seen couples gliding across shiny dance floors, moving as one to the fluid sounds of a melodious orchestra. That's what I wanted to do. I wanted us to be Fred Astaire and Ginger Rogers.

We signed up for our six-week dance class, but instead of gliding around the room, we learned to make boxes with our feet. I quickly became bored with the "slow, slow, quick, quick," squares and asked the instructor if we could move around the room a bit. So she taught us how to make a box with its lid open: two steps sideways and two steps forward.

Actually, Steve moved forward and I had to move backward. This seemed unfair to me. Why did I have to be the one to move backward? Now, I understood that we couldn't both move forward. We would be on a collision course for certain. But why me?

The instructor assured me that this was the way God had planned it and told me to stop complaining. (She didn't say it exactly like that, but that's what she meant.)

After a few dance lessons, I didn't look at all like Ginger Rogers. Actually, I resembled Fred Rogers. We were not gliding around the room, moving as one. It was as though Steve were pushing a shopping buggy around the mirrored dance floor.

I use the word "push" because I wasn't guided easily. More than once the instructor tapped me on the shoulder and said, "Mrs. Jaynes, you're leading again."

After a while I did learn how to give in to the gentle pressure of Steve's hand on my back to move me forward and the release of the pressure to move me back. With a slight tug I learned when to twirl, and with a lift of the arm, I learned to spin. Amazingly, I discovered that Steve had the most difficult job as leader of the dance. He had to learn when and where to push, press, and release, and all I had to do was follow his cues. When I did, I looked like the one doing all the fancy moves, but in reality, I was just following his lead.

What a lesson God taught me about the symbiotic dance of marriage. When I learn to comply with my husband's leadership, we move as one in a beautifully choreographed dance designed by God.

Biblical Submission

As we have already seen, God created man and observed, "It isn't good for man to be alone." So He created a helper for him. We are designed for a unique purpose. God created us to be and do many things, but being leader of the home is not one of them.

Does that mean we are inferior? No. Does that mean we are incapable of leadership? No. Does that mean we aren't as smart?

No. It simply means we have a different role in the marriage union.

The apostle Paul wrote: "Wives, submit to your husbands as to the Lord. For the husband is the head of the wife as Christ is head of the church, his body, of which he is the Savior" (Ephesians 5:22-23).

The word "submission" comes from a combination of words that mean "to arrange under." It was primarily a military term. Even though we are to submit one to another, God is a God of order, and He has set up the following chain of command in the home: Wives submit to husbands, who submit to Jesus, who submits to God. This does not mean that the husband is a dictator and the wife is a doormat. Remember, Ephesians 5:25 tells the husband to love his wife as Christ loved the church and gave His life for her. That doesn't sound like any dictator I've ever known. That sounds like sacrificial love.

Why do we women struggle so with the issue of submission? I think it goes back to the Garden of Eden. We've already established that God created woman as unique and with specific roles, but man was given the role of leader. Note that just a few verses after God created Eve, she's already taking the lead, disobeying God, and dragging a rather weak Adam along with her. Because of Adam and Eve's disobedience, they both received curses from God. One of the curses or judgments placed on Eve was "Your desire shall be for your husband, and he shall rule over you" (Genesis 3:16).

Some commentators say this verse refers to sexual desire. But as my husband would say, "That would not be a curse! That would be a blessing!" No, I think "desire for your husband" means that woman will desire to *control* her husband or *rule* over him. It was part of the curse, and she's been trying to rule over him ever since. The idea of man ruling over woman has been a thorny issue ever since too.

All Christians are called to a life of submission. Ephesians 5:21 says: "Submit to one another." We are to set aside our selfish desires and serve each other.

I saw a very disturbing picture this week in the newspaper. A baby had been born with two heads. From the top of the skull another head had developed. It was horrendous. I imagine that when God looks at our homes and sees the same deformity in leadership, He turns His head in disgust. God is a God of order, and His plan is stated plainly in 1 Corinthians 11:3: "But I want you to understand that Christ is the head of every man, and the man is the head of a woman, and God is the head of Christ" (NASB).

> *My wife (who is the woman of my dreams) defers to me even though sometimes she doesn't agree. —Patrick* (This wife is a lawyer—author's notation.)

> *Though submission is important to me, what is much more important is the spirit of that submission. Just as God doesn't merely want our ritualistic obedience but rather our hearts, so it is with my desire for my wife. Her enjoyment of me (in sex, in submission, in counsel, in play, in work, etc.) is my greatest motivator. Another way to say this is that if she is merely "willing," then I am much less likely to be "able," if you know what I mean. —Allen*

> *I wish my wife understood that submission is a turn-on! —Stu*

> *One of our greatest struggles has been with disciplining the children. My wife rarely lets me have the last word or make the final decision. —Dean*

Kim learned the difficulty of trying to lead when no one will follow. "For several years, I was vice president of a small company," she explained. "The president had to step down for two years for personal reasons, and I stepped into her shoes until she was ready to return. The entire staff was made up of women, and it was my responsibility to lead this group, make final decisions, and cast the vision for future growth. After about two weeks, I discovered the difficulty of trying to lead the women in one unified direction. Everyone had their own ideas and agendas. Each decision was a major battle. Many times, when I made a final decision on a controversial topic, someone would continue to bring it up again until I was worn down and conceded to her desires.

"I watched my leadership skills wane and my confidence plummet. After two years of constant struggle trying to fulfill my appointed responsibilities, I gave up emotionally. *What's the use,* I thought. *They're going to do what they want to anyway.*"

After two years, Kim resigned her position.

Kim had experienced, firsthand, the struggle many men face in their marriages. They know God has called them to be the leader of the home, and yet the struggle to fulfill that call isn't worth the effort and hassle. After years of being shot down, put down, and run over, many men sit down with the remote control in one hand, a drink in the other, and a "whatever" attitude toward their once exciting and fulfilling marriage.

Just as men are called to be the head of the home, the wife is called to be the heart of the home. When we are acting as the head, it is hard to be the heart.

Her Way or the Highway

Here's an excerpt from a very disturbing and embarrassing newspaper article titled, "Marriage? It's Her Way or the Highway":

> If you want your marriage to last a long time, the newest advice from psychologists is quite simple: Be willing to do what your wife says.

A widely recommended form of marital relationship advice has been active listening, in which one partner paraphrases the other partner's concerns—"So what I hear you saying is…" But that is unnatural and requires too much of people who are in the midst of emotional conflict, says psychologist John Gottman of the University of Washington. "Asking that of couples is like requiring emotional gymnastics," he says.

Gottman and his colleagues studied 130 newlywed couples for six years in an effort to find ways to predict both marital success and failure. Couples who used techniques such as active listening were no more likely to stay together than couples who did not, they report in the latest *Journal of Marriage and the Family*, published by the National Council on Family Relations.

"We need to convey how shocked and surprised we were by these results for the active listening model," the team admitted in the article. In fact, Gottman and his colleagues have long recommended active listening to couples seeking counseling and had expected that its use would be a predictor of success in marriages.

That it was not a predictor, he said, suggests that its widespread use in marital counseling should be abandoned.

The marriages that did work well all had one thing in common—the husband was willing to give in to the wife.[1]

Does that bother you? It certainly bothers me, and I'm sure it bothers God. To think that the success of a marriage depends on the husband giving in to the wife's demands? Isn't that what Adam did with Eve?

Sheldon Vanauken in his book *Under the Mercy* tells about four women who made an incredible discovery about the results of submission. These four women were meeting for a weekly Bible study and came across the passage in 1 Corinthians 11:3 about the husband being the head of the wife, and they were faced with a decision.

> The leader for that evening read the verse aloud, paused, and read it again...Every one of those women—they all knew it—was head in her marriage.
>
> Someone said weakly, "Does St. Paul say anything else about headship and submission?" An index was consulted, and the other Pauline statements (Colossians 3:18; Ephesians 5:22; 1 Timothy 2:11) were read out. There was some discussion. Finally the leader said, "Well, girls—what do we do?" Someone else said, "We've got to do it."
>
> ...Then came the miracle. In less than a year the four women, with amazement and delight, were telling each other and every other woman they knew what had happened. The husbands, all four, had quietly taken over...and, with no exceptions, every one of the women felt her marriage had come to a new depth of happiness—a joy—that it had never had before. A rightness.
>
> Seeing this astonishing thing that not one of them had thought possible...the four wives one day realized an astonishing further truth: They realized that their husbands had never demanded and would never have demanded the headship; it could only be a free gift from wife to husband. [2]

The woman of my dreams understands that submission to the man as the leader of the home does not make her less; in fact, the Proverbs 31 woman is lauded and exalted for this very reason: She is fully submitted and fully vested in the role of helping her husband and her family. She uses far more than just her cooking, cleaning, and bedroom skills. She is creative, diligent, productive, and content. Talk about a superwoman. —Bob

I wish my wife respected me as leader of our household and didn't try to take her role and mine. I want to fill my own shoes. My wife has enough to do without my stuff. —John

The woman of my dreams is one who will always share her thoughts and emotions freely, in discussion or in conflict, but lives in submission to her husband's decisions—always ready to help when mistakes are made. —Thomas

The woman of my dreams is not a doormat but makes her opinions known. She also knows that a man is accountable to God for the family. —Eric

One of the biggest struggles in our marriage has been conflict resolution. We never seem to see eye to eye on things. Plus, she is so dominant in her personality that she backs me into a corner, either emotionally or physically. —Eric

But what if we know he's wrong? He may very well be wrong, and if he is, he's responsible to God for that decision. The greater *right* is to submit—the greater *wrong* is to demand our own way. If we submit to a decision and it fails, that's when we have the opportunity to serve up love on a silver platter. Imagine the husband who hears this response to his failure: "Well, Paul, we prayed about this and made the best decision we could with the information we had. Now let's think about what to do next." Notice the "we" in that response. Listen, he knows he failed—a loving wife will try to make him not feel like a failure.

Perhaps your husband is not a Christian. Do you still submit to his authority? As long as he is not telling you to do something immoral or illegal, the general rule of thumb is yes. Time and time again I have seen men who have come to Christ because of the gentle spirit of their wives. Peter wrote: "Wives, in the same way be submissive to your husbands so that, if any of them do not believe the word, they may be won over without words by the behavior of their wives, when they see the purity and reverence of your lives" (1 Peter 3:1-2). Linda's gentle spirit combined with prayer is what we saw in chapter 3 that drew Buck to Christ.

If your husband is not a Christian, submission does not guarantee he will come to faith. You may do everything in your power to become the wife of your husband's dreams, and he may act as though he doesn't even notice. But I can promise you this, dear one, God notices. He is watching you and is well pleased. When you meet Him face-to-face, He will embrace you in His arms and say, "Well done, good and faithful servant" (Matthew 25:21).

SEVEN

Wanting What You Have vs. Having What You Want

Steve and I were sitting in the hot seat in front of our couples Sunday school class. Each week the teacher interviewed one couple in the class to learn what made their marriage a success. Steve and I knew in advance the questions she was going to ask, but we had not discussed our answers.

I sat in anticipation of the last question, perched on my high-backed chair (or, should I say, "pedestal"). I was already feeling myself becoming puffed up by the accolade that was sure to proceed from Steve's lips. The final question was, "What is one thing you admire most about Sharon?" I dreamed he would say, "The way the light shines on her silky chestnut hair" or "That special twinkle in her dark blue eyes."

I held my breath as Judy posed the climactic question.

Steve paused. "She's thrifty," he finally answered.

"Thrifty!" I echoed in disbelief. "You've got to be kidding!"

The class broke out in laughter at my disappointment in Steve's answer. Oh well, not so romantic after all. From the time we met, Steve has known that I am very thrifty. We met and married when we were poor college students and had to have a yard sale to take a honeymoon. After we graduated, I still enjoyed saving money and searching for bargains. He has always appreciated the fact that I've been content with whatever state we are in.

Interestingly, I wrote an article for *Crown Ministries* magazine about Steve's response in Sunday school. One man wrote me a note. "Be encouraged," he said, "I am sure that because you are thrifty, your husband doesn't have to work so hard and has more time to look at the light shining on your chestnut hair and gaze in your blue eyes." He understood the secret joy of the husband of a contented wife.

One way a wife can show respect for her husband is by being content with their financial situation. When she is dissatisfied with his provision for the family and constantly pushes for more material possessions, she is telling him he is failing to provide in the manner to which she had *hoped* to become accustomed. The woman of his dreams is more than satisfied...she is thankful for his hard work and tells him so.

One man told me, "I feel like when I walk in the door, I might as well just hand over my paycheck. And on top of that, I never feel like it's enough. She always wants more."

Comments such as "I'm tired of always having second best" or "When will we ever be able to afford..." or "I'd be happy if I had..." are arrows that pierce the heart and soul of a man. He longs to be a good provider for his family. He wants to be the hero for his bride. He wants to feel appreciated. However, what I heard from my respondents is that many feel their paychecks are never enough.

In America, the average size of a new home has grown from 1500 square feet to 2190 square feet, and the number of cars has risen from one car for every two Americans to one car for each driving-age individual.[1] The number of people taking cruises each year has risen from 500,000 to 6.5 million, and the production of recreational vehicles has risen from 30,000 to 239,000.[2]

Does this mean that we are happier and more satisfied? Journalist Kathy Bergen notes, "A growing body of research is reaching the conclusion that the country's unprecedented surge in affluence is not spawning a corresponding surge in content-ment, personal or societal."[3] Robert E. Lane, professor emeritus of political science at Yale University, notes that there's a general "spirit of unhappiness and depression haunting advanced market democracies" (that's us). He goes on to say we're experiencing a rising tide of clinical depression and that Americans are no happier than we were when our incomes were one-third of what they are now, back in 1948.[4]

One of the wealthiest men in the Bible, King Solomon, concluded this about the accumulation of wealth as it relates to contentment: "I have seen all the things that are done under the sun; all of them are meaningless, a chasing after the wind" (Ecclesiastes 1:14). Are we, as wives, causing our husbands to chase after the wind to make us happy, when in reality material gain is not what is going to make us happy at all?

The one couple in all eternity that had the makings for complete contentment were Adam and Eve. And yet Satan came to Eve and told her there was more. He made her think God was holding out on her and tempted her with the one restriction put on her by God. As I've said before, Satan is not very creative, but he's very effective. He comes to us the same way he came to Eve. He makes us think, *There's more...God's holding out on me.* And before you know it, we're sinking our teeth into the bitter fruit of discontentment and dissatisfaction.

Paul understood contentment. He wrote: "I have learned to be content whatever the circumstances. I know what it is to be in need, and I know what it is to have plenty. I have learned the secret of being content in every situation, whether well fed or hungry, whether living in plenty or in want. I can do everything through him who gives me strength" (Philippians 4:11-13). Amazingly, Paul wrote these words when he was in prison chained to a Roman guard.

Mr. Davis received a call from his credit card company. "Mr. Davis, we are happy to report we have located the man who stole your credit card."

"Oh, that's nice," Mr. Davis replied.

"But, sir," the operator continued, "it appears your card was stolen three months ago. Why didn't you report it?"

"That's easy," Mr. Davis replied. "The man who stole the credit card was putting less on it than my wife, so I just let it go."

> *One of the biggest struggles in our marriage is money management. Just stick to the budget. See the big picture and learn that you don't have to have it all right now. I know the stats about finances and divorce, and they should tell us how important this issue is in a marriage. —Brad*

> *Our greatest struggle has been finances and not telling the truth about the finances…trying to keep up with the culture. —John*

EIGHT

A Picture Paints a Thousand Words

I am about to tread on thin ice with some of you ladies, but there's no use skating around the issue. Dr. Willard Harley Jr., author of *His Needs, Her Needs,* states that each man has five basic needs in a wife: sexual fulfillment, recreational companionship, an attractive spouse, domestic support, and admiration.[1] Sandwiched right in the middle of a man's five basic needs is a topic we'd like to ignore, but we can't ignore it anymore than we can ignore the peanut butter in a peanut butter sandwich. A man wants the woman of his dreams to be attractive.

God created men and women very differently. Men are visually stimulated and enjoy looking at a pretty woman. Your husband's greatest dream is that woman will be you. Don't blame him for the way he is wired. You'll have to take that issue up with God, who made him.

This need to have an attractive spouse may be difficult for many women to understand because we simply aren't wired that way. Women are attracted to men who are caring, sensitive, loyal, and fun. Sure, it doesn't hurt if they are handsome as well. But when it comes to long-term relationships, women are much more drawn to inner qualities. A man is also drawn to treasured inner qualities, but usually not until he can enjoy the packaging as well.

An Outward Expression of an Inward Respect

Why in the world do I have a chapter about man's desire for an attractive spouse in this section on respect? Because when we decide that we don't care how we look, we are in essence telling our husbands that we don't care about them. We are disrespecting his needs and desires. Too many of us ladies went to great pains to be attractive to hook the man of our dreams and then, once we reeled him, we let our looks drift out to sea. Unfortunately, when our personal appearance runs amuck on the shores of complacency and laziness, so do our marriages.

"But he should love me for who I am on the inside!" I hear women say. You know what? He probably does. However, I have to remind us once again that men are created to be visually stimulated. They like to look at pretty things, and what they really want to look at is the wife of their dreams.

I suspect for most of us, maybe 99.9 percent of us, our husbands were initially attracted to us because of our appearance. If we took extra care to catch that man of ours, why would we stop taking extra care to keep him? Many of us are banking on the fact that our husbands are too "spiritual" to be shallow enough to lose interest because we've let ourselves go. If that's the case, you might be writing some bounced checks.

> I am embarrassed to say this, but my wife has gained a lot of weight since we married. Not a little weight. A lot. I love her, but I feel insulted that she doesn't want to take better care of herself for me. I feel angry at times that she thinks it's superficial for me to want her to look nice. I don't know if she even realizes it's a struggle in our marriage, but I pray often that I

can find her attractive with an extra hundred pounds on her. —Bill

The woman of my dreams takes pride in herself and works to maintain her health in order to be desirable and attractive while aging gracefully into maturity, not seeking youth, but wisdom, grace, and inner beauty. —Tom

The woman of my dreams understands that how she looks is important to me. —Bob

"But I can't look like Catherine Zeta-Jones!" you may be saying. Let me ask you this: Did you look like Catherine Zeta-Jones when he fell in love and married you? Probably not. Then he's not asking you to look like Catherine Zeta-Jones now. Your man simply wants you to look your best for him! He wants you to make the effort to resemble the woman he fell in love with, not a glamorous movie star. We don't have to have the perfect body, perfect hair, and perfect complexion, but it would be nice if more than our fingerprints and eye color resembled the girl he married.

"What do you think men look at first when they see a woman? If you answered 'her body,' you are wrong. According to a *USA Today* survey, 39 percent of men say the first thing they notice are eyes. Next highest (25 percent) is smile or teeth. Only 14 percent say the first thing they notice is the body."[2]

"What kind of body do you think attracts men? Do you think men prefer the lithe supermodel look? No. The average man finds normal-weight women sexier than very thin women. This was the conclusion of Dr. Devendra Singh, University of Texas psychologist, after showing pictures of twelve female shapes to seven hundred men."[3]

What can we learn from those two bits of information? Having a physical appearance that is pleasing and appealing to our husbands does not necessarily mean being thin or voluptuous. It does mean that we take care of our appearance and look our best for him.

Our culture has a fascination with eternal youth and beauty. Please hear me—that is not what I am endorsing here. I am racing toward 50 years old faster than a speeding bullet. My skin is sagging, my wrinkles are creeping, and my flat plain of a tummy has been transformed into a "mound of wheat" as King Solomon so affectionately called it (Song of Songs 7:2). That's life.

What I am saying is to not let your appearance go after you say "I do." Continue (or begin) to exercise and maintain good muscle tone and burn calories, wear your hair in a way that is pleasing to him, experiment with makeup to accentuate your positive facial features, and dress in ways that make your husband proud.

Now, I know my friends are wide-eyed seeing me mention the benefits of exercise. That is something I have fought tooth and nail for years, but as my "mound of wheat" has continued to mound with age, I've had to concede and put on my walking shoes.

Friend and author Janey McHenry noticed that she had two areas in her life that were going lacking: exercise and prayer. So she decided to combine the two and start "prayer walking." She prays as she walks. This has worked well for me.

Find an exercise program you're comfortable with and begin to get those muscles moving. It may be a gym with child-care, a church jazzercise program, the YMCA, a kickboxing video, or simply a brisk walk through the neighborhood. If exercise is a problem for you, find a friend or accountability partner to exercise with you. When I walk with a friend, I tend to walk longer and the time passes more quickly. That exercise partner could be your husband!

How's your wardrobe? Is it early American housewife frump? Baggy jumpers, nappy sweats, and tattered tennis shoes? Pick up a catalogue and ask your husband what he'd like to come home to and think of sprucing up a bit.

How's your hairdo? *What do?* you may be saying. Don't just cut your hair short because it's easy to maintain. Ask your husband what hairstyle he prefers. (My husband wrote that last sentence, but not all men like long hair.)

I read a quote that said, "A woman takes a husband thinking the man she has chosen can be changed. A man takes a wife thinking the woman he has chosen will never change." Go back and look at your wedding pictures. How are you doing?

I know this goes against what so many are saying in the church. I even wrote a book titled *Ultimate Makeover: Becoming Spiritually Beautiful in Christ*, which emphasizes the importance of inner beauty. The truth is, no amount of makeup, weight loss, or designer clothing can make a woman who is unattractive on the inside be truly beautiful. Beauty begins on the inside and works its way out. However, the truth remains that the woman of your man's dreams is attractive. She's not necessarily a beauty queen, but she is someone he can be proud of.

Being attractive is not trying to become someone you are not. It is doing the best with what you have. It is amazing what a dab of lipstick, a stroke of blush, a stylish haircut, and a smile can do for a woman's appearance. There are very few women who are naturally beautiful—most require a little help. But remember, beauty is a package deal. It involves more than physical features. Our smile, style, walk, talk, hair, flair, clothes, countenance, posture, and polish all combine to make a beautiful woman.

On bad hair days, my sister-in-law, Pat, always says, "Just smile and nobody will notice your hair." You know what? She's right! So few people wear a smile these days that it's refreshing to see one. I bet your husband would love to see you wearing one more often!

Paul reminds us, "Do you not know that your body is a temple of the Holy Spirit, who is in you, whom you have received from God? You are not your own; you were bought at a price.

Therefore honor God with your body" (1 Corinthians 6:19-20). I think even the Holy Spirit might enjoy a fresh coat of paint and some new wallpaper every now and then. He might appreciate it if we'd keep the pipes running well, beams from sagging, and the attic clear of too much clutter!

Have you ever noticed how a man who enjoys hunting likes to display his catch? A great blue marlin is mounted over a mantel, a five-point deer head emerges from a wall, a stuffed greenhead mallard proudly tops a desk. All this is to say, "Hey, guys, look at what I caught. Eat your heart out."

There's nothing your husband would like more than to flaunt his attractive wife out in public. He may not mount you on the wall (let's hope not), but when he walks into a room with you at his side, he wants to say, "Hey look what I caught. She's all mine. Eat your heart out!" I daresay, when you walked down the aisle on your wedding day, that's exactly what he was thinking!

"When a man has an attractive wife, it says he has the appeal and talent that deserve someone of her caliber. When a man's wife lets herself become unattractive, the message comes across loud and clear that he couldn't get someone better and probably deserves her. He has little to offer, the world decides, and he attracts little in return."[4]

The Bible reminds us that "man looks at the outward appearance, but the LORD looks at the heart" (1 Samuel 16:7). The truth remains…man looks at the outward appearance.

Many women go back to the Proverbs 31 woman in their defense. "Charm is deceitful and beauty is vain [or fleeting], but a woman who fears the LORD, she shall be praised" (Proverbs 31:30 NASB). We can't get off that easily. Let's go back and learn a bit more about the wife of noble character. "She selects wool and flax and works with eager hands" (verse 13), which means she made nice clothes for her family. "All of them [her family] are clothed in scarlet" (verse 21), which indicates that the cloth was of high quality. She herself is clothed in "fine linen and purple" (verse 22), which is associated with nobility. Purple dye was very hard to come by in those days and was usually reserved for royalty. While she may not have had a closet full of clothes from the mall, the Proverbs 31 woman made sure that her clothes were attractive and of high quality. That does not sound like a woman who gave little attention to her appearance. Besides, if she didn't care about her appearance, I don't think her husband would have been sitting around the city gates bragging about her to his friends.

An added benefit of a woman taking care of her appearance is that she will feel good about herself, have more confidence, and exude energy. Men often say that a smiling, confident woman is very attractive!

There's an old adage that a picture is worth a thousand words. What is your picture in the mirror telling your husband about how much you respect him? Spending time to take care of your appearance is not selfish. Quite the contrary. If you are married, it is selfish not to.

> *The woman of my dreams is attractive and takes good care of herself.* —Stan

> *A man wants a woman he can feel proud to have on his arm and who loves only him. I remember while we were courting that I told her on my arm was where I always wanted her, and that still holds true today.* —Norman

NINE

Happy Endings

Over the past several years I have come to love two words in the Bible as never before. Those two words? "But God." I want to take you back to the beginning of this section on respect and revisit Don and Jona. Even though Don and Jona were officially divorced, God was not finished with either of them. God took Jona to a place of repentance and began to soften, remold, and remake her heart. That's what God does. He doesn't try to cover up our flaws; He starts from scratch and makes us new. And though the divorce was final, God was only just beginning to work on Jona's heart.

"God took me to a place of repentance," Jona explained. "For the first time, through a support group, I saw clearly what I had done to destroy my marriage. I had always blamed our problems on Don changing jobs so often, but the real problem was my lack of respect for the God-appointed leader of my home. I was the problem, and Don simply couldn't take it anymore. I had rejected him with my words, my appearance, and my withdrawal from physical touch."

Whether or not God would salvage the marriage, Jona made a commitment that she would allow God to salvage her.

Jona's heart longed to be reunited to Don, but her ultimate goal was to become the woman God wanted her to be. She immersed herself in Bible study and prayer, and began to take an interest in her appearance. Interestingly, as the pounds began to drop, so did the scales that had covered her eyes.

"I began to understand what God's Word said about the relationship between a husband and wife. I was not Don's Holy Spirit. I was not the leader of my home. God had called me to respect Don as the leader, to honor him as a child of God, and to love him with my all. One day when Don came to pick up our two boys, I shared with him what I had been learning.

"I told Don I knew that we were divorced, but I was making a commitment to submit to him. I didn't when we were married, but I was going to from that time forward."

"That's fine," he told me. "But you need to know I'm moving on with my life."

"You can move on," I said, "but I'm staying right here."

Jona continued to encourage Don and give him her BEST.

"BEST stands for bless, edify, share, and touch," she explained.[1] "I began to touch him when he came by the house. I'd pat his back or give him a quick hug. When I knew he was coming, I'd put on a nice dress and fix my hair. I'd tell him I was proud of how he was handling the boys and share with him what God was teaching me. Some people told him I was trying to trick him and that he should ignore me. But it wasn't a trick. God had changed my heart and I was committed, no matter what happened between us in the future, to never go back to being that bitter woman I had been before.

"I hate to admit this, but for the first time I prayed for Don. I had never prayed for him before, but now I pray for him all the time."

Jona lost 100 pounds and gained a beautiful glowing countenance. It was amazing. More than the change in her physical appearance, the glow of Jesus Christ shone through her radiant face.

One day Don said, "Jona, you look soooo good."

"Don, I know I look better, but what I want you to see is my heart."

"I do see it, Jona," he said with tears in his eyes. "But I'm moving on."

Jona knew that Don had met someone else, and while she never said a discouraging word about his new relationship, she continued to love Don and give him her BEST. When her mind went to the other woman, God whispered, *You don't need to know the details. Leave that to Me. You just love him.*

Don was confused at times and a bit leery of the change. "Why do you think I'm wonderful, all of a sudden?" he asked her.

"Because now I see you through God's eyes," she explained. "I see that you are a wonderful man."

One night Jona sat down and wrote Don a letter.

Dear Don,

People have been encouraging me to write you a letter as a way of expressing my feelings and emotions to you. Also, as a way of bringing a healing effect to a very hurtful relationship. So here I am writing this to you at 2:37 a.m. on Monday morning, March 17…

I want to say that I am truly sorry for the hurt and pain I've caused you. I have been in such a place of pain myself and have always just "thrust" upon you the hurt I've known in these later years. So many of the circumstances over the last ten years caused me to turn and blame you for the failings caused by our bad circumstances.

After Mother died I was in so much pain I began to run from you…Most people would have been drawn closer to their spouse because of such a traumatic experience, but I became depressed. I looked around and the way seemed hopeless and bleak. I was looking to you to "fix" it. I was hoping you would come to my emotional rescue and pick me up from the darkness I was feeling. I also looked at all the things you weren't doing and began to dwell on them. I wanted so much to have everything be okay, but it wasn't. I became more and more depressed. Then I thought *I* could "fix" it and began to challenge everything you did…just to prove I could do it and handle it. I didn't want your strength…I didn't want your involvement…I pushed you away, thinking, *He can take it. He's a man!* I thought my husband could take anything. Let's just see how much he can take. Can he feel the pain I'm in…let's just see. The more I hurt, the more I placed upon you. I began to think of you as inhuman. I didn't stop to think that what I was doing caused you hurt and pain. "Don can take this. He's strong and he believes everything is an opportunity." "Let's give him lots of opportunity to prove how much of a husband he is." I waited…I watched…I criticized…I belittled…I rejected…I disrespected. "After all, Don can take anything…he is strong."

I blamed God and it showed. I quit going to church. I withdrew from Him. In turn, I withdrew from you. I blamed you and quit giving to you. I turned on the children and quit being a mom. I turned on myself and quit living! I wanted to die because I felt dead inside. Everything around me was dark and cold and stale. I began to feel pain, physical pain, and my body began to deteriorate. You saw this and couldn't understand. We were at two different places and couldn't seem to help each other. I kept waiting for you to pull me up, and you were probably waiting for me to pull you up. Neither one of us could help! What a place to be at when no one could rescue us…

I believe I have now come to the point of saying…Don, I am truly sorry for the lack of respect I have given to you over the years. I am sorry for not trusting in you and for not believing in you as a man and as a husband. I have wronged you, and for this I am deeply and remorsefully sorry. I do not wish to cause you any further pain or sorrow, and I vow to hold to the promise of not disrespecting you anymore. You are a man of worth and of value…You are a man of character and of honor. You are a man of God. It has now come time to say, "God's will be done. To God be the glory."

You said you don't know what the future holds. I, too, don't know what that future looks like, but I trust in God and He will see us through. Our marriage may never be reconciled, but our relationship can be. I'm going to continue to trust in God no matter what happens. No matter how hard or how difficult. He is now my Protector, my Rock, my Comforter, and my Life!

Don fell in love with Jona all over again. No, it wasn't a trick—it was a miracle. God has given them a second chance. They were remarried on August 24, 2003. Oh, how I love Him…He is the God of second chances.

Dear friends, Jona has so graciously allowed me to tell you her story because she has decided that she will do anything to help even one woman not make the same mistakes she has made. She cried and cried all through the recounting of the story and relived the pain…for you. "God allowed me to go to a terrible place," Jona explained. "My prayer is that others will not have to go to that place before they wake up and realize what they are doing to their men."

Respect. It is key to becoming the woman of his dreams.

Twenty-Five Ways to Show Respect

1. Do not talk down to him.
2. Do not talk badly about him to others.

3. Do not check behind him to make sure he did something to your standards.
4. Do not disregard his wishes.
5. Do not ignore his requests.
6. Do not laugh at his mistakes.
7. Do not make him the brunt of your jokes.
8. Do not compare him to other men.
9. Do not complain about your finances or his ability as a provider.
10. Do not speak sarcastically or with verbal jabs.
11. Do not roll your eyes when he makes a comment you do not agree with.
12. Do not continually "have a better idea."
13. Do talk to him in a pleasant tone.
14. Do speak highly or compliment him in front of others.
15. Do allow him to do tasks his own way and then thank him when he is finished.
16. Do value his opinions.
17. Do support his decisions.
18. Do try to fulfill his requests.
19. Do thank him for providing for your family.
20. Do allow him to make final decisions.
21. Do support him in his decisions, regardless of the outcome.
22. Do avoid the words, "I told you so."
23. Do take care of your appearance.
24. Do ask his opinion about your clothes or hairstyle.
25. Do tell him you are proud of him.

Section Three

Adores Him

TEN

The Longing of His Heart

It was a beautiful sunny day in Peoria, Illinois. Excited about the bouquet of surprises she had planned for her husband, Jill had slept very little during the night. As the first rays of sunshine peeped through the blinds, Jill quietly climbed out of bed and tiptoed into the kitchen. Moments later, she reappeared to awaken her prince with a kiss on his stubbly cheek and the aroma of waffles filling the room.

"Good morning, sunshine," she whispered. "Happy thirtieth birthday."

"What's this?" Jeremy mused.

"Breakfast in bed for the birthday boy," Jill replied.

Jeremy and Jill had been married for three years, and a recent move from Charlotte, North Carolina, to Peoria, Illinois, was a reminder that no matter what circumstances they faced in life, they moved as one. Jill had waited 31 years for the man of her dreams, and on this day she was once again overwhelmed with the gift God had given her in Jeremy.

After Jeremy finished his breakfast, Jill handed him a stack of note cards tied with red ribbon. The top card read "Jeremy Charles Tracey, here are 30 ways you are wonderful."

"Okay, now for your next surprise," Jill explained.

Jeremy gingerly removed the ribbon and began to read the cards.

"You are wonderful because you love the Lord."

"You are wonderful because you are handsome and sexy."

"You are wonderful because you are funny."

"You are wonderful because you are a great listener."

"You are wonderful because you make other people feel special."

"You are wonderful because you are talented and creative."

"You are wonderful because you are a great provider."

"You are wonderful because you are a wonderful son."

Through laughter and tears, Jeremy read the cards aloud—one-by-one. Each card became a jewel in his birthday crown.

"I don't want to go to work today," Jeremy said as he hugged his bride. Little did he know the surprises that awaited him throughout the day.

Jeremy walked into his office to discover a list on his desk. Across the top it read, "Thirty treasured memories." Then he proceeded to read a list Jill had compiled of thirty of their favorite memories. Again, through laughter and tears, Jeremy read each entry and allowed his mind to recall and relish each event.

An hour before Jeremy's shift was over at the radio station where he worked, Jill showed up with a duffle bag in tow.

"You're early," Jeremy noted as he glanced at the clock.

"Not today, big guy," Jill replied. "I've arranged for another DJ to finish your shift and you're comin' with me."

Jeremy was then ushered to a back room and ordered to change into shorts and a T-shirt. When he came back out, Jill said, "Okay, now close your eyes. I have another surprise."

"What more can you do to make this day special!" Jeremy laughed.

"Just close your eyes."

"They're closed."

"Now open!" Jill squealed.

"John, what are you doing here?" Jeremy yelled.

"I couldn't let my buddy celebrate his thirtieth birthday without me," the surprise guest replied.

The two men embraced. Jill cried.

One thing Jeremy missed most after his move to Illinois was his best friend, prayer partner, and Sunday school teacher, John Rinehart. Jill had arranged for John to fly to Peoria to share their special day. It was a tremendous surprise and one Jeremy would never forget.

Jeremy's birthday was filled with surprises and acts of love, both big and small. At the end of the day, when Jill snuggled up beside her prince in bed, he held her tight and let the tears trickle down his face onto hers.

"I have never had even one surprise in all my birthdays. I still can't believe all you went through to make this day special." He then cupped her face in his hands and whispered, "You love me so much."

"You better believe I do," Jill smiled. "That's why I did all this…you are so special to me. I adore you."

One of your husband's greatest longings is to be adored, admired, and appreciated by the woman of his dreams. Too many times we walk down the aisle with a striking resemblance to Snow White, but then somehow we turn into the wicked queen. If that's the case in your home, fear not! The story's not over yet. We can draw a line in the sand and say "No more." Like Jona in chapter 9, we can make a commitment to adore our husband and give him our BEST (bless him, edify him, share with him, touch him). Let's take a look at how your husband can echo Jeremy's sentiments as he lays his head on the pillow at night… "You must really love me."

> *I earn a good six-figure income and work hard so my wife doesn't have to work outside the home—but I rarely feel appreciated. Instead, I feel like a nuisance because I might occasionally make a floor dirty or leave a cup out. —Jim*

The one thing that could make our marriage better is for my wife to appreciate and encourage me—but we've talked about that many times and I'm afraid it's not going to change. —Jack

I wish my wife understood how hard I work for my family to provide for them. I long for more physical attention—hugs, hand holding, sitting close. —Ben

I wish my wife understood how important being appreciated is. —Curt

The Triple-A Club of Marriage: Adoration, Admiration, and Appreciation

The woman of your man's dreams adores, admires, and appreciates him! She thinks he is the most wonderful man to walk the earth. He's brave and brilliant, loving and logical, tough and tender, handsome and humorous, masculine and magnificent, sexy and savvy…why, she just can't say enough about all of his wonderful attributes. That's the stuff of your man's dreams.

What does it mean to adore your husband? Basically, it means to love him with all your heart…and let him know about it. George Eliot once said, "I like not only to be loved, but to be told I am loved." Do you want to see your husband's face light up like a full moon? Tell him you are amazed that he knows how to _____, or that you are impressed by his _____, and then sit back and watch him glow. You become the mirror in which your husband sees himself.

One day Anabel Gillham was sitting on the deck of a vacation spot doing her needlework. Her thimble slipped off her finger, dropped through a crack in the boards, and disappeared into the lake. She went into the cabin, rummaged around until she found another thimble, and went back to her sewing. This time, her husband, Bill, was sitting on the deck with her. The thimble came off again, hit her leg, and was heading for the water. Bill reached out from his chair, picked the thimble out of the air, and handed it back to her.

"Your coordination just amazes me," she said, smiling.

"I just love that kind of stuff," he beamed.

When Bill told that story at one of his Lifetime Guarantee seminars, a man came up to him and said, "Man, if my wife would say things like that to me, I'd dive in after that other thimble!"[1]

> *The woman of my dreams is one who treats me like the king of my castle, yet still knows she is the queen and is not afraid to confront me when she sees that I need some direction. —Randall*

> *What one thing I wish the woman of my dreams understood? That I just want to be admired and respected. —Bill*

> *The woman of my dreams loves spending time with me. She hugs me, kisses me, and she initiates sex. —Stan*

Where Does He Go to Feel Admired and Appreciated?

Where does your husband go for admiration and appreciation? He goes somewhere. All men do. Does he go to work in hopes of hearing "job well done"? Does he go to the ball field in hopes of hearing "way to go, man"? Does he go back home to mother to hear "I'm so proud of you, son"? Does he work late in hopes for a few compliments from the gals in the office? Does he feast on compliments from patients or clients? Does he hang out at the gym flexing and building his biceps? Tell me, where does your man go to be admired?

In my first job as a dental hygienist, I noticed how the all-female staff as well as the patients admired the doctors in the building where I worked. I admired them too! They were a wonderful group of very talented men who were gifted and skilled in their chosen profession. As a young girl in my early twenties, I wondered how the doctors' wives felt about the praise their hubbies received all day long.

Amazingly, a few years later, I had the opportunity to find out for myself. After working for two years, I decided to go back to college to get a bachelor of science degree. While there I met and married Steve Jaynes, a young dental student. When he started his practice, I remembered the admiring women from years before, and I made a commitment that of all Steve's admirers he would have from the day he opened his practice until the day he retired, I was going to be his number one fan!

Dr. Willard Harley says,

> When a woman tells a man she thinks he's wonderful, that inspires him to achieve more. He sees himself as capable of handling new responsibilities and perfecting skills far above those of his present level. That inspiration helps him prepare for the responsibilities of life. Admiration not only motivates, it also rewards the husband's existing achievements. When she tells him that she appreciates him for what he has done, it gives him more satisfaction than he receives from his paycheck. A woman needs to appreciate her husband for what he already is, not for what he could become, if he lived up to her standards. For some men—those with fragile self-images—admiration also helps them believe in themselves. Without it these men seem inherently more defensive about their short-

comings…While criticism causes men to become defensive, admiration energizes and motivates them. A man expects—and needs—his wife to be his most enthusiastic fan. He draws confidence from her support and can usually achieve far more with her.[2]

If you have been withholding admiring words from your husband, it may feel strange to begin. First and foremost, be authentic—be real. If you contrive admiring words, he will be able to tell. Start with one compliment or a word of appreciation. It may be as simple as "thank you," and soon the admiration will begin to flow. Who knows? It may begin to flow both ways.

Dr. Harley also notes,

> Remember that a man really needs appreciation. He thrives on it. Many men who come to me because they have had affairs stress that the admiration of their lovers acted as a warm spring breeze in comparison to the artic cold of their wives' criticism. How can they resist? Don't make your husband go outside your marriage for approval; he needs the perspective your appreciation gives him. That does not mean you have to fake it with him and tell him you love something that drives you wild, but work with him on the needs you must both fulfill, setting up a strategy that builds admiration.[3]

Not all men are admired at work. If work is a place where your husband meets opposition at every turn or leaves feeling like a failure, he will search for someplace to be admired. It could be on the softball field, on the racquetball court, as a deacon at the church, or in an online chat group. How wonderful when that place is in your heart, in your arms, in your home.

In his book *Twenty Surprisingly Simple Rules and Tools for a Great Marriage*, Dr. Steve Stephens lists four types of compliments. One type is a compliment of *possession*, such as, "I love that sweater." The second type is a compliment of *appearance*, such as, "That sweater brings out the blue in your eyes." The third type is a compliment related to *behavior*. It might be something such as, "That was very sweet to let that car go in front of you today." And the fourth type of compliment is one of *character*, such as, "Someone asked me what the definition of integrity was, and my mind immediately went to you."

Look for ways to give compliments every day. Pay attention to your husband and take note of his appearance, behavior, and character qualities. Then sprinkle a few compliments his way. For some, your husband may become confused or seem skeptical with this sudden showering of praise. He may say, "What's up with the compliments all of a sudden?"

If that is his reaction, just say, "I'd forgotten what a wonderful man I'm married to and I'm realizing it more and more every day!"

If you have been doling out a steady dose of criticism, sarcasm, and verbal jabs, you have a lot of weeds to pull. As a matter of fact, some deep-rooted weeds have a tenacious way of sprouting up time and time again. You may have to continue to apply weed killer (words of admiration) for many years before the life-choking weeds are all gone.

> *The woman of my dreams is feminine and lady-like. She puts on makeup and is presentable when I get home, even if we don't have anyplace to go. My wife is really good at this.* —Robert

> *The woman of my dreams is excited to see me every night when I come home from work.* —Dave

*My wife is always full of praise for me when I give
her gifts or surprises. This makes me feel appreciated.*
—Paul

Roman Rules

In chapter 3, we looked at 1 Corinthians 13 as a model for
prayer. Sometimes we read those familiar verses and almost hear
the angels in the background as if the words should be sung
instead of lived. But they are not simply symbolic prose. They are
stern words, difficult words, a call for reevaluation and self-
examination. Am I loving my husband well? Am I adoring the
man God has given to me? Am I admiring him as a child of God?
Am I appreciating him for who he is today instead of what he
could be if he lived up to my expectations? Am I giving my heart
freely, or do I make him feel as though he constantly has to earn
my love?

Paul gives us some good advice on how to love one another in
Romans 12:9-18.

- Love must be sincere.
- Cling to what is good.
- Be devoted to one another.
- Honor one another above yourselves.
- Never be lacking in zeal.
- Be joyful in hope.
- Be patient in affliction.
- Be faithful in prayer.
- Share with God's people who are in need.
- Practice hospitality.
- Bless those who persecute you.
- Rejoice with those who rejoice.
- Mourn with those who mourn.

- Live in harmony with one another.
- Do not be proud.
- Do not be conceited.
- Do not repay anyone evil for evil.
- Be careful to do what is right in the eyes of everybody.
- If it is possible, as far as it depends on you, live at peace with everyone.

Now take a look at that list. It is easy to think that Paul is talking about our friends or fellow Christians. But if these are the guidelines for loving our friends, how much more are they guidelines for loving our very own husbands! As Ann Landers once said, "Love is friendship that has caught fire. It is quiet understanding, mutual confidence, sharing, and forgiving. It is a loyalty through good and bad. It settles for less than perfection and makes allowances for human weaknesses."[4]

> *I think many Christian men feel like they can never measure up because expectations of Christian women are so high. My wife doesn't compare me to other men—she compares me to James Dobson!* —Pete

> *The woman of my dreams would adore me. She would look up to me and make me feel strong and virile. I know this sounds old-fashioned in this day and age, but my ideal wife would not be self-sufficient. She would need me.* —Phillip

> *I wish my wife understood how much I long for attention and interest from her.* —Dave

The Five Love Languages

What says "love" to one person may not say "love" to another. Dr. Gary Chapman, author of *The Five Love Languages*, suggests that we each have a certain "language" that speaks love.

1. *Words of Affirmation:* Compliments, words of encouragement, and requests rather than demands affirm the self-worth of your spouse.

2. *Quality Time:* Spending quality time together through sharing, listening, and participating in joint meaningful activities communicates that we truly care for and enjoy each other.

3. *Receiving Gifts:* Gift are tangible symbols of love, whether they are items you purchased or made or are merely your own presence made available to your spouse. Gifts demonstrate that you care, and they represent the value of the relationship.

4. *Acts of Service:* Cooking a meal, ironing a shirt, keeping the house clean, and paying the bills all speak volumes of love to the man whose love language is acts of service. If this is your man's love language, he will become frustrated when certain household duties go undone and will feel like a million bucks to sit down to his favorite meal.

5. *Physical Touch:* Physical touch is more than sexual. It is holding his hand, touching his shoulder, giving him a hug, patting his back, or snuggling next to him while watching TV.[5]

Ask your husband what says love to him. You may be surprised. You may think that keeping the house clean or cooking yummy meals says love when what he really wants is quality time or words of affirmation. If he can't tell you what his love language is, ask him what he longs for or wishes he had more of.

ELEVEN

Love on a Silver Platter

Sarah had been working the night shift at the hospital for seven days straight. On this, her first day off, she was enjoying her third cup of coffee and perusing a crisp new magazine. It was nice having a day when no one needed her attention. *I think I'll watch an old movie,* she thought to herself. But as Sarah attempted to place the video into the machine, she noticed that a cassette was already in there. She pressed eject and stared wide-eyed at the video that emerged. Her heart raced and her emotions were an amalgamation of rage and disappointment. She reached for her car keys with the video in hand and stormed to her husband's office.

"Randy," she said through clenched teeth. "Look what I found in the VCR this morning! While I was at work, you were supposed to be keeping an eye on the boys. Apparently, Brad rented a porn film and watched it after you went to bed. Look at this!" she screamed. "An X-rated movie about a teenage orgy! Just what are you going to do about this? He is going to be grounded for life! Just wait until I get my hands on him!"

What Sarah did not notice was the ashen appearance of Randy's face, the downcast eyes, and the beads of perspiration forming on his forehead. Finally, he held up his hand to stop his wife's tirade.

"Sarah," he quietly spoke. "The movie isn't Brad's. It's mine."

Sarah and Randy are Christians. They serve in the church working with the youth and have led various Bible studies through the years. Sarah could not have been more crushed had a Mack truck appeared out of nowhere and run its three-ton cargo over her heart.

What does the wife of his dreams do in this situation? What would you do? What did Sarah do? How does a woman continue in her marriage after such a betrayal? How does a woman forgive the man who has pledged to love her for the rest of her days?

Forgiveness. It's a tough subject. However, we will never be the wife of his dreams without it.

Let me say something right from the beginning. As I begin this chapter on forgiveness, I in no way want us to think that forgiveness means turning a blind eye to a problem that needs attention. Pornography, alcoholism, drug abuse, and a plethora of other addictions must be addressed and dealt with for any marriage to survive and thrive. A wife is not doing her husband any favors by allowing such behavior to continue. To ignore such behavior is to enable sin to deposit droplets of poison into a man's soul.

So what did Sarah and Randy do? They went before the elders of their church. Randy admitted his sin, joined a support group for men addicted to pornography, and meets weekly with an accountability partner who asks him tough questions. He has installed a program on his computer that tracks the sites he visits and a report of Internet history is sent to his accountability partner and his wife weekly.

Yes, they took steps to deal with Randy's sin, but one of the greatest steps of faith occurred when Sarah decided to forgive and trust him again. Was it difficult? You bet. Was it impossible? Not through Christ.

> *The woman of my dreams understands that what a man wants is a true living example of God's love.*
> —John

> *Describe the woman of my dreams? Okay, she needs patience and lots of it! Understanding and love go a long way too. Please forgive me more often… that's really all I ask!* —Ron

> *The woman of my dreams is one who is graceful in her demeanor, words, and deeds. She is one who is not judgmental, does not hold a grudge, and does not continue to bring up past mistakes.* —Eric

The Problem of Unforgiveness

C.S. Lewis said, "Everyone says forgiveness is a lovely idea until they have something to forgive."[1] I wholeheartedly agree. Forgiveness can be especially difficult when the man who promised to love and cherish you all the days of your life is the one who hurt you. But what is more difficult is to have the marriage of your dreams without it. Unforgiveness is a spider that will suck the very lifeblood from your relationship. Paul wrote, "I have forgiven in the sight of Christ for your sake, in order that Satan might not outwit us. For we are not unaware of his schemes" (2 Corinthians 2:10-11). Other Bible translations say: "We are not ignorant of his devices" (KJV) and "We are not ignorant of his wiles and intentions" (AMP). Satan does a happy dance when we are wronged, but he throws an all-out celebration when we don't forgive. He knows that as long as we hold a grudge, our earthly example of Christ and the church (our marriage) will be marred and we will never experience the oneness God intended.

In his book *What's So Amazing About Grace?* Philip Yancey said, "If we do not transcend nature, we remain bound to the people we cannot forgive, held in their vise grip. This principle applies even when one party is wholly innocent and the other wholly to blame, for the innocent party will bear the wound until he or she can find a way to release it—and forgiveness is the only way."[2]

Henry and Richard Blackaby explain, "Bitterness has a tenacious way of taking root deep within the soul and resisting all efforts to weed it out…Time, rather than diminishing the hurt, only seems to sharpen the pain…You find yourself rehearsing the offense over and over again, each time driving the root of bitterness deeper within your soul…Bitterness is easy to justify. You can get so used to a bitter heart that you are even comfortable with it, but it will destroy you. Only God is fully aware of its destructive potential."[3]

Only God is fully aware of the destructive potential of unforgiveness to tear a marriage apart. Unforgiven offense by unforgiven offense, brick by brick, walls are built that separate husbands and wives emotionally, physically, and spiritually. Perhaps you are unsure if you have unforgiveness in your heart. Perhaps the unforgiveness has been there for so long that it feels at home in your heart and you don't even realize it's there. Stop and pray Psalm 139:23-24: "Search me, O God, and know my heart; test me and know my anxious thoughts. See if there is any offensive way in me and lead me in the way everlasting." If God brings something to your mind, deal with it quickly and completely.

A group of computer experts came together to try to decide whether computers ought to be referred to as male or female. Like sailors who refer to their ships as "she," the programmers didn't want to call their beloved machines an "it." The females gathered in one room and the males in another. The women decided that computers should be referred to as "he" for the following reasons:

1. In order to get their attention, you have to turn them on.

2. They have a lot of data but are still clueless.

3. They are supposed to help you solve your problems, but half the time they are the problem.

4. As soon as you commit to one, you realize that, if you had waited a little longer, you could have had a better model.

The men, on the other hand, thought that they should be referred to as "she" because:

1. No one but their creator understands their internal logic.

2. The native language they use to communicate with other computers is incomprehensible to everyone else.

3. As soon as you make a commitment to one, you find yourself spending half your paycheck on accessories for it.

4. Even your smallest mistakes are stored in long-term memory for later retrieval.

Ouch! I think the men's number 4 really hits home. I say we learn how to press the delete button and even empty out the trash bin. Let there be no recycling of the deleted files, and pray we aren't smart enough to figure out how to retrieve them from the hard drive!

I always tell ladies who are trying to get organized to clean out their closets with three bags: a put-away bag, a throw-away bag, and a give-away bag. I also emphasize that it is important to use bags you cannot see through. Why? You're smiling, I can tell. We tend to go back through the trash and pull things from the bag. "That sweater isn't so bad...out it comes. I haven't worn that belt in ten years, but you never know...out it comes." We tend to pull things out of the trash with our marriages as well. I encourage you to let it go. It's simply cluttering up your marriage with stuff you don't need.

Deciding to Forgive

The first step to forgiveness is prayer. The Bible tells us to pray for our enemies. I hope your husband is never your enemy, but I can assure you, on some days you may feel as though he is. So let's follow God's instruction and pray for him. "[Prayer] is a gentle tool of restoration appropriated through the prayers of a wife who longs to do right more than be right, and to give life more than to get even."[4] It may not turn your husband's hardened heart to putty in your hands, but it will melt the hardness of resentment in your own.

God is love. That's just who He is. When you pray for your husband, each prayer plants a tiny seed full of potential. What a joy to watch the Holy Spirit water those seeds and produce a bumper crop of forgiveness and love.

With any wound comes pain. It can be as small as a pin prick or as large as an anvil falling on your head, leaving you reeling for days trying to regain your balance. One option is to hide the hurt, stuff it down, and act as though nothing happened. That will only work for so long, until the pent-up pressure causes a volcano of emotion to erupt with the hot lava of anger spewing over onto everyone around you. Just as a physical injury causes a bruise or a wound, an emotional injury causes a wound as well. It may be small, but even a bump can cause great pain when the soul is jabbed in the same spot time and time again.

What do you do with the wounded soul? I can assure you amputation is not the answer. I know of no one who would amputate an injured leg or arm without first trying every conceivable means to bring about healing. Why then do we so readily amputate our marriages? Amputation may not be divorce, but a cutting off emotionally from the other person. For many couples, forgiveness is the first step to bringing life back into the marriage.

The word "forgiveness" in Greek is *aphieme*, and it means "to let go from one's power, possession, to let go free, let escape."[5] It means to take someone off your hook and place them on God's hook. It is a decision and not a feeling. Does forgiveness mean that we are saying what the person did was not wrong after all? Quite the contrary. It means we are letting them go free regardless of the offense. It is an act of grace—giving a gift that is undeserved.

Paul wrote, "One thing I do: Forgetting what is behind and straining toward what is ahead" (Philippians 3:14). Forgiveness is making a commitment to look ahead and leave the past behind. This requires a refusal to bring up the offense that has already been forgiven. Someone once said, "There's no point in burying the hatchet if you're going to put up a marker on the site."[6]

"Forgiveness is God's invention for coming to terms with a world in which, despite their best intentions, people are unfair to each other and hurt each other deeply...He (God) began by forgiving us. And he invites us all to forgive each other. Forgiving is love's toughest work, and love's biggest risk. If you twist it into something it was never meant to be, it can make you a doormat or an insufferable manipulator. Forgiving seems almost unnatural. Our sense of fairness tells us people should pay for the wrong they do. But forgiving is love's power to break nature's rule...It is forgiving that supplies the healing stream of long-term tomorrow."[7]

Forgiveness has little to do with what was done to us, but much to do with what we choose to do with it. I believe it is the ultimate expression of love.

Think of Jesus' last words on the cross. He was betrayed by one of His disciples, abandoned by His best friends, and condemned to die by the very people who had hailed Him with palm branches just a few days before. Jesus was falsely accused, publicly humiliated, shamefully spat upon, mockingly crowned, mercilessly flogged, and cruelly nailed to a Roman cross. And yet, with His last breaths He prayed, "Father, forgive them, for they do not know what they are doing" (Luke 23:34).

What depth of love! I can barely begin to comprehend it. When I think of how much God has forgiven me, how can I not forgive in return?

> *A man wants to be respected, not put down or kicked for all his mistakes. He wants respect in public as well as in private. —Eric*

Asking for Forgiveness

Now, what if you are the one who needs forgiving? Dear sisters, nothing can be more healing to a marriage than for the guilty party to admit she is wrong and ask for forgiveness. Jesus stressed the seriousness of reconciliation when He said, "Therefore, if you are offering your gift at the altar and there remember that your brother has something against you, leave your gift there in front of the altar. First go and be reconciled to your brother; then come and offer your gift" (Matthew 5:23-24).

As you read the pages of this book, you may realize there are several areas where you have wronged your husband. Like Jona in chapter 9, perhaps you may need to write your husband a letter, admitting your mistakes and asking for his forgiveness. You might consider the following:

1. Tell him specifically why you were wrong.

2. Let him know that you are sorry for hurting him.

3. Ask him to forgive you. Say the words, "Will you forgive me?"

4. Tell him what you are going to do differently.

The word "repent" means to say you're sorry, turn, and go in the opposite direction. While your husband may forgive you, what he wants to see is that you are "turning in the opposite direction" and will not hurt him again. Trust is something that must be reconstructed once it is destroyed. Don't become angry if he waits to see a change before he begins to trust you with his heart again.

Robert Quillen said, "A happy marriage is the union of two good forgivers."[8] There is much truth in that.

Letting Go for Good

Here is a visual exercise in forgiveness adapted from Anabel Gillham's book *The Confident Woman*. Take a helium-filled balloon to an open field. With a felt-tip pen, write a word or a few words that denote what you are forgiving your husband of. Then pray, "Dear Lord, today I am forgiving _____ for _____. No longer will I hold this over his head. Never again will I bring this up. I am cutting him loose. You tell us to cast all our cares on You, and today I am giving You this burden I have been carrying around for quite some time. As I watch this balloon disappear, please remove any resentment or bitterness from my heart. In Jesus' name, amen."

Then, release the balloon and watch it drift into the very presence of God. Every time the thought of that offense returns to your mind, remember that you have given that to God.

Perhaps you and your husband both need to release a balloon. Here's what one woman wrote to Anabel:

Dear Anabel,

This past Tuesday my husband and I purchased two helium balloons (one pink, one blue) and then drove up into the mountains. We found a good lookout point and parked. We both sat for a long time, writing all over our balloons. Al didn't read what I wrote, and I didn't read what he wrote.
I was the first to let mine go. The wind was blowing odd, sort of down into the valley. The balloon tangled in the tree branches, blew loose, and after the third tree, broke wildly toward the sky!

Then Al let his balloon go—in a different spot to avoid the trees—but one got his too. I walked over to the tree; put both hands on the trunk and shook it. The balloon caught the wind and took off toward the heavens.

That's a good picture of what this circumstance has been for us, Anabel—a real struggle to let it go, to make it fly.

I "feel" more free than I have felt in years, and when the negative thoughts do come, I close my eyes and see those pink and blue balloons going and going…and I know it's all right.

God has everything in His hands.[9]

Perhaps you have a balloon that needs to be released to God. Perhaps it would be a wonderful outing for the two of you to do together.

TWELVE

Serving in a Me-First Society

For years I've heard the phrase that marriage is a 50/50 proposition. But the question is, who gets to decide when one spouse has hit the halfway mark? "It is impossible," notes author and marriage expert Dennis Rainey, "to determine if your spouse has met you halfway because neither of you can agree on where 'halfway' is. Each is left to scrutinize the other's performance from his or her own jaded perspective."[1]

Carley and Dan are a couple who have gone the extra mile...to not go the extra mile. They constantly keep score as to who put a new bar of soap in the shower last or who refilled the toilet paper roll last or who opened the new tube of toothpaste last. "It's sort of a contest to see who can use the smallest sliver of soap or use the last, last drop of toothpaste," Carley boasted. The contest, as silly as it may seem, boils down to who is going to serve the other. Imagine how adored Dan would feel if Carley began to get out a new bar of soap before the sliver war began or replenished the toilet paper before it was totally out?

If you want to try a contest in your home, how about seeing who can out-serve the other! The apostle Paul encouraged us:

> Don't just pretend that you love others. Really love them. Hate what is wrong. Stand on the side of

good. Love each other with genuine affection and take delight in honoring each other (Romans 12:9-10 NLT).

Let's stop and think about Jesus' last days with His disciples before the crucifixion. I imagine that His mind was racing with last lessons He wanted to make sure His followers understood before He ascended to heaven. On their final night together, as they were eating the Passover meal, Jesus "got up from the meal, took off his outer clothing, and wrapped a towel around his waist. After that, he poured water into a basin and began to wash his disciples' feet, drying them with the towel that was wrapped around him" (John 13:4-5). When He finished washing their feet, He put on His clothes and returned to His seat. " 'Do you understand what I have done for you?' he asked them. 'You call me "Teacher" and "Lord," and rightly so, for that is what I am. Now that I, your Lord and Teacher, have washed your feet, you also should wash one another's feet. I have set you an example that you should do as I have done for you' " (John 13:12-15).

Can you imagine the disciples' awe as their Lord and Master took on the role of a servant and stooped to wash the mud and dust from their filthy feet? I can understand Peter's cry of protest.

When Jesus washed the disciples' feet, it wasn't simply a nice act of kindness. He was actually fulfilling a need that the others had refused to meet. It was customary in those days for the host of a dinner party to have a servant wash the guests' feet. There were no Reeboks or Nikes in those days. Men and women wore leather sandals as they walked the dusty, sometimes muddy, roads of the Holy Land. Nothing felt better than to sink calloused, throbbing feet into a cool basin of water and rinse away the cares of the day. However, on the occasion of the Last Supper, there was no servant available to wash the guests' feet and no one volunteered.

So God-made-man wrapped a towel around His waist and did what no one else was willing to do. Afterward, He sat down and said, "Now you do it too."

Jesus calls each of us to serve one another. It seems we are much more agreeable to serving our friends than serving our husbands. And yet, when we serve our husbands, we are in effect serving Christ Himself. "When you do it unto the least of these, you do it unto me," Jesus said.

Have you ever had those days when you said, "I've had enough. It's time for him to take care of me. I wash the clothes, pick up the clothes, cook the meals, buy the groceries, vacuum the floors, dust the furniture, scrub the bathrooms, and pay the bills. That's it. I'm not doing another thing to 'serve' this man. I am not a servant, by George."

Connie Grigsby wrote this comical but convicting story for our magazine, the *P31 Woman*.

> There it was. The suitcase. Standing at the top of the basement stairs. The very sight of it made her angry. Her husband had just returned from a business trip and had left the suitcase sitting there, assuring her that very soon he would take it downstairs and put it away.
>
> A week later the suitcase was still there. Because the laundry room was in the basement, she was forced to step over the suitcase time and again as she did the laundry. Before long, the way she treated her husband was directly related to the number of times she stepped over the suitcase. It was the middle of January, and outside the temperature was dropping rapidly. Inside, it was plummeting as well.
>
> One day she decided to move the suitcase. No, she didn't take it downstairs and put it away. Helping was the last thing on her mind. Instead, she carried it into their bedroom and put it in the middle of the floor where her husband walked, effectively blocking his path to the bed.

Now he would see firsthand how irritating it was to arrange one's life around a misplaced suitcase.

She returned to the kitchen expecting to feel a certain amount of satisfaction and relief. She felt neither. Nor did she feel the least bit smug. What she felt was an overwhelming sense of sadness and grief. She knew her husband had not intentionally left the suitcase out; he had simply forgotten about it. Yet even knowing that, she clung to her "right" to feel offended and hostile.

She stood in the kitchen and thought about the suitcase. Had it belonged to guests, she would have happily taken it from their hands and insisted on putting it away herself. So why, she wondered, was she unwilling to help her husband in the same way? Why was it so much easier to serve others than it was to serve him? She took a good long look at herself and didn't like what she saw. No wonder she felt grieved. Something needed to change, all right, and it had nothing at all to do with the suitcase.[2]

Does something about this story strike a familiar chord within you? Do you find serving others more pleasant than serving your spouse?

The following is a lengthy passage, but I want you to read it with your husband in mind. God calls us to serve one another. That includes our husband and precludes every other human relationship.

> If you have any encouragement from being united with Christ, if any comfort from his love, if any fellowship with the Spirit, if any tenderness and compassion, then make my joy complete by being like-minded, having the same love, being one in the spirit and purpose. Do nothing out of selfish ambition or vain conceit, but in humility consider others better than yourselves. Each of you should look not only at your own interest, but also to the

interests of others. Your attitude should be the same as that of Christ Jesus. Who, being in the very nature of God, did not consider equality with God something to be grasped, but made himself nothing, taking the very nature of a servant, being made in human likeness. And being found in appearance as a man, he humbled himself and became obedient to death—even death on a cross! (Philippians 2:1-8).

Do nothing out of selfish ambition. Hmm.

Do nothing out of vain conceit. Hmm.

In humility consider others better than yourselves. Hmm.

Look out for the interests of others. Hmm.

In Philippians 2:4, Paul tells us to look out for the interests of others, not just for our own. "Look out for" is from the Greek word *skopos*, from which we get the words "telescope" and "microscope." It means to pay close attention.[3] Whether we are using a telescope to get the big picture or a microscope for close examination, the wife of your man's dreams pays close attention to the needs, desires, dreams, joys, and sorrows of her man. She looks closely at his heart and absolutely adores him.

"We need to be clear that servanthood doesn't mean the bondage of slavery. As Jesus put on the towel and served his disciples, he proved to us conclusively that God's kind of serving love flows from choice not coercion, from strength not weakness, from gladness not guilt. It's positively liberating."[4]

Jesus said, "Give, and it will be given to you. A good measure, pressed down, shaken together and running over, will be poured into your lap. For with the measure you use, it will be measured to you" (Luke 6:38). It may be entirely possible for you to serve your husband and not feel that you are receiving anything in return. However, your heavenly Father is always watching, and the measure you use to bless your husband will be used by your heavenly Husband to bless you in return.

My wife discovers what I like and dislike and then anticipates from there. This could come in the form of being the person who writes checks and balances the books to surprising me with peanut butter chocolates whenever I'm not looking. —Steve

One thing my wife is really good at is that she doesn't nag, and, boy, do I appreciate that! She is not a doormat. She's a tiger and doesn't mind standing her ground with me or anyone if need be. There is a difference between nagging and disagreeing. —Brad

I long to hear my wife tell me some nice sweet words. —Barumbya

Phillips Brooks wrote, "Duty makes us do things well, but love makes us do them beautifully."[5]

THIRTEEN

Romance Is Not Just for Us Girls

If there is one thing I know about us girls, it's that we like romance! We love romance novels, romance comedies, romance tragedies, and romance, romance, romance. We'd much rather take in a romantic movie than an action film, and what woman doesn't dream about her man romancing her the way he did when they were dating? But guess what? That man of yours longs for it too.

One night Steve and I were planning a romantic evening at home alone. We borrowed a video from our friends Gene and Sherrie. *A Vow to Remember* promised to be a real tearjerker. The couple on the video sleeve appeared lost in each other as their arms intertwined in a lovers' embrace, and the back cover boasted, "Capture your mind, your heart, and your soul…Paints a compelling picture of forever love."

The lights were dim, the candles were lit, and the mood was set. However, when Steve placed the video in the machine, we were not greeted with strains of a melodious theme song or misty eyed romance. Oh no. It was Arnold Schwarzenegger with machine gun at the ready! Our romantic evening was rudely interrupted by *RoboCop*. Gene had placed the wrong movie in the video sleeve!

Perhaps romance in your marriage has a greater resemblance to *RoboCop* than *A Vow to Remember*. If so, let's rewind and remember those days when love was new.

In *The Romance Factor*, Alan McGinnis notes, "Being an artist at romance does not require so much a sentimental and emotional nature as it requires a thoughtful nature. When we think of the romantic things, we think of events that occur because someone made a choice to love. A man stops off at a florist and brings his wife a single rose in the evening, a girl makes her lover a lemon pie with just the degree of tartness he likes, a wife makes arrangements for her husband to take the caribou-hunting trip he thought he'd never afford—these are not the goo of sweet emotion. They are the stuff that comes from resolution and determination, and they are strong mortar."[1]

Here are twenty-five ideas to romance your man:

1. Put a chocolate kiss in his briefcase.
2. Draw a candlelight bath and invite him to join you.
3. Surprise him in the shower.
4. Warm up his towel in the dryer.
5. Warm up his socks in the microwave.
6. Greet him when he comes out of the shower with a warm towel and a steaming cup of coffee.
7. Watch the sunset together.
8. Eat by candlelight.
9. Take ballroom dance classes.
10. Spray a mist of perfume on his pillow.
11. Place an "I love you" sign in a public place. (I put a sign outside Steve's office window to surprise him on Valentine's Day. The fact that all his patients saw it was an extra bonus!)
12. Write him a love letter.
13. Write him a poem.

14. Write an acrostic of reasons you adore, admire, and appreciate him A to Z.
15. Have a special song.
16. Fax a love note to him at the office.
17. Send him a romantic e-mail.
18. Leave an "I love you" message on his voice mail.
19. Kidnap him for an overnight getaway. (Pick him up at the office. Have his overnight bag packed and kids stowed away at a friend's.)
20. Celebrate your first date, first kiss, and the day he asked you to marry him.
21. Write him a thank-you note for something specific he did for you.
22. Make a video of your life together using old photographs and your favorite songs. (There are companies that will do this for you. You supply the photos and the songs.)
23. Make a list of 25 reasons why you adore him.
24. Give him a trophy for "Best _____." Trophy shops will engrave anything you like!
25. Give him a full-body massage, telling him what you like about each body part as you move along.

We'll get into more ways to bring romance back into your marriage in the last section of the book.

I wish my wife understood how important it is for a man to feel like he has made the mark. —*Bart*

The woman of my dreams is pretty (not beautiful). She has fun pampering me and is always affectionate. —*Herman*

The woman of my dreams understands how fragile a man's ego is. —*Paul*

FOURTEEN

Lost that
Lovin' Feelin'?

What do you do when you've lost that loving' feelin'? Maybe you truly adored your husband in the beginning, but now you can't remember why. Maybe you honestly admired his finer qualities, but now you can't remember what they were. Maybe you deeply appreciated his wonderful attributes, but you can't see them now. What do you do? Here's a statistic you might find interesting. According to an analysis of the National Survey of Families and Households, 86 percent of unhappily married people who stick it out find that, five years later, their marriages are happier. In fact, nearly 60 percent of those who rated their marriage as unhappy in the late 1980s, and who stayed married, rated their same marriage "very happy" or "quite happy" when reinterviewed five years later.[1] In comparison, those who divorced and remarried divorced again at a rate of 60 percent.[2]

So, starting over may very well be the answer! As long as it's with the same man.

Remember and Return

In the book of Revelation, God had this to say to the church at Ephesus: "Yet I hold this against you: You have forsaken your first love" (Revelation 2:4). Ephesus was one of the most loving churches in the New Testament and yet somewhere along the way they lost that initial thrill of knowing Christ. Their love for each other and for God had grown cold.

As I read God's lament, I whispered a prayer. "Oh, Lord, how many of us women have forgotten our first love? We've forgotten the thrill we felt when we first met our husbands—the spine-tingling chills when he walked into a room, the heart-skipping flutter when he called on the phone, the tender wooing when we opened a letter penned by his hand, the electricity of sexual desire stirred with a kiss. Somewhere between taking out the garbage, paying the bills, running the carpool, mowing the lawn, disciplining the kids, and folding the laundry—somewhere among the mundane routine of life—we've lost the romance."

How do we get it back? God gave the church two simple steps for the Bride of Christ to renew her passion for her Beloved, and I believe we can apply the same principles to renewing our passion for the man of our dreams.

Step 1: Remember

Step 2: Return

Remember what drew you to your husband in the first place? Remember how you tried to please him, capture his heart, and win his affection? That may have been 50 pounds and a full head of hair ago, but that young man who longed to be adored, admired, and appreciated still lives within his heart. He wants to know if he still "has what it takes." Let him know that he does.

Everyone loves a love story. Tell your children the story of how you first met and fell in love. Remember special days such as your first date, your first kiss, or when you first realized he was the man you wanted to marry. On your anniversary, listen to a tape or watch a video of your wedding. Steve and I celebrate not only our wedding anniversary but also the day he asked me to marry him. I'm sure our son has tired of hearing the story time and time again, but he's never doubted that his parents are crazy about each other.

I wish my wife would kidnap me for a romantic holiday...which we have never done. I'd settle for going to bed earlier so we wouldn't be so tired and coming to bed with no clothes on! —Zack

The wife of my dreams admires me and gives me lots of praise. —Adam

I think women need to understand just how critical it is that a husband feels like his wife's hero. —Harry

A man finds his value in accomplishments. I think a man feels more fulfilled when his wife shows and tells him how much she appreciates all he does and shows and tells him how much he means to her. —Dave

Martin Luther once said, "Let the wife make the husband glad to come home, and let him make her sorry to see him leave."

Song of Songs

In the Song of Songs, the bride drenched her beloved in words of admiration. Perhaps you would like to write such a song of your own.

How handsome you are, my lover! Oh, how charming! And our bed is verdant (1:16).

Like an apple tree among the trees of the forest is my lover among the young men. I delight to sit in his shade, and his fruit is sweet to my taste (2:3).

Strengthen me with raisins, refresh me with apples, for I am faint with love (2:5).

My lover is radiant and ruddy, outstanding among ten thousand. His head is purest gold; his hair is wavy and black as a raven. His eyes are like doves by the water streams, washed in milk, mounted like jewels. His cheeks are like beds of spice yielding perfume. His lips are like lilies dripping with myrrh. His arms are rods of gold set with chrysolite. His body is like polished ivory decorated with sapphires. His legs are pillars of marble set on bases of pure gold. His appearance is like Lebanon, choice as its cedars. His mouth is sweetness itself; he is altogether lovely. This is my lover, this my friend (5:10-16).

Now, you give it a try and write a love song of your own.

A husband wants to know that he is the man of his wife's dreams. At least I do. I wish my wife treated me with respect and attention the way she did when we were dating—looking nice, smiling, and being patient and kind. —Dan

My wife is very good at saying "thank you" for helping out or supporting her. —Russ

The woman of my dreams lets me know in plain English what she appreciates about what I do for her and the family. —Dave

How Do I Love Thee?

How do I love thee? Let me count the ways.
I love thee to the depth and breadth and height
My soul can reach, when feeling out of sight
For the ends of Being and ideal Grace.
I love thee to the level of every day's
Most quiet need; by sun and candle-light.
I love thee freely, as men strive for Right;
I love thee purely, as they turn from Praise.
I love thee with the passion put to use
In my old griefs, and with my childhood's faith.
I love thee with a love I seemed to lose
With my lost saints—I love thee with the breath,
Smiles, tears, of all my life!—and if God choose,
I shall but love thee better after death.

—ELIZABETH BARRETT BROWNING

Twenty-Five Ways to Show
Your Husband You Adore Him

1. Let him hear you thank God for him.
2. Hug him several times a day.
3. Always sit by him at gatherings.
4. Kiss him several times a day.
5. Ask him if there's anything you can do for him today.
6. Write love notes on the bathroom mirror or shower wall with soap.
7. Smile at him.
8. Wink at him.
9. Have a special song.

10. Start each day with a kiss.
11. End each phone conversation, no matter how brief, with "I love you."
12. Don't interrupt when he's telling a story.
13. Compliment him in front of others.
14. Compliment him in private.
15. Make his favorite dinner often.
16. Say "please" and "thank you."
17. Praise him in front of his peers.
18. Praise him in front of his family.
19. Praise him in front of the children.
20. Write him notes based in truths from Scripture, such as: "You are a dearly loved child of God." "You are God's masterpiece." "You are salt and light in the world."
21. Praise him for something specific that he did well.
22. Compliment him in front of the children.
23. Make a list of 25 qualities you admire about him.
24. Tell him you appreciate his hard work.
25. Make him a coupon booklet with items that can only be fulfilled by you. I'll let you come up with the ideas.

Section Four

Initiates Intimate Friendship with Him

FIFTEEN

A Thousand Sharings

There he sat, cross-legged on the floor at Bible study, dressed in slightly worn Levi's and a red flannel shirt with sleeves rolled up midway on his muscular forearms. His dark brown eyes and strong jaw line combined to form a picture of masculinity and sincerity. He was a third-year grad student with a well-worn Bible, and he seemed too good to be true.

When I had become a Christian as a teenager, I made a commitment to not become "unequally yoked," as Paul described in 2 Corinthians 6:14. I resolved that I would marry a Christian or not marry at all. The problem was that most of the Christian young men I met weren't any fun. They were nice enough, but there were no sparks and no excitement. (Remember, these are the musings of a teenager!) So I predicted I would marry a nice, pleasant, drab Christian man. I would probably like him okay, but I didn't hold out much hope for a passionate, exciting relationship. I resolved myself to a peaceful yet boring life.

When I saw Steve Jaynes for the first time, my heart truly skipped a beat. When he asked me out on a date, it just about stopped altogether.

"Sharon, would you like to go out with me Friday night?" he asked.

"I'd love to," I answered.

"Great. There's a missionary from Mississippi I want to hear. I'll pick you up around 7:00."

As he turned to walk away, I thought, *Okay, Lord. He's cute, smart, Christian, and no fun. Boring, boring, boring.* Not that going to listen to a missionary speak isn't inspiring, but it was not my idea of romance.

When Steve came to pick me up, I wasn't quite ready. My roommate made small talk with him as an oldies station played beach music in the background. When I walked into the room, Steve asked, "Do you like that kind of music?"

"Yes, I love it!" I answered.

"I do too. I have an entire collection of oldies beach music. Do you know how to shag?" (The shag is an East Coast dance much like the swing.)

"Yep. I've been shagging since the sixth grade."

"Let's see if we do it the same way," he said as he grabbed my hand.

We took a spin around the den and then headed out the door to hear the missionary. After the lecture, we dashed to a favorite college spot and danced the night away. I remember praying that night, "Lord, can it be that this wonderful man is also fun? Will there be passion and excitement after all?"

I image God was enjoying a good laugh at the pitter-patter of His little maidservant's heart that evening. God truly is able to give us exceedingly abundantly more than we can ever ask or think (Ephesians 3:20). He certainly did when He gave me Steve. He is the spiritual leader of my home; he is my lover; and he is my friend.

Intimate Friendship

What do you think of when you hear the word "intimate"? Perhaps sexual relations come to mind, but true intimacy involves much more than a physical union. It is a joining of two hearts through mutual sharing…being "naked and unashamed." My dictionary defines intimate as *being familiar, very private and personal, warmly personal, resulting from close study.* It is common knowledge that women enjoy this type of friendship, but I was pleasantly surprised that intimate friendship with the woman of his dreams is a longing of a man's heart as well.

> *I really don't know if there is anything that I wish my wife understood better about me. She knows me like a book because she takes the time to know me.* —John

> *The biggest struggle in our marriage has been spiritual, emotional, and physical intimacy. She had a difficult time being vulnerable.* —Richard

> *I wish my wife understood my inner life better: insecurity, embarrassment, shame, hope.* —Gene

> *I don't think there is anything my wife doesn't understand about me. We are able to openly talk about everything.* —Nathan

While the word "intimacy" means sex to some, sexual fulfillment *begins* with intimate friendship. Marriage expert John Gottman wrote, "The determining factor in whether wives feel satisfied with sex, romance, and passion in marriage is, by 70 percent, the quality of the couple's friendship. For men, the determining factor is, by 70 percent, the quality of the couple's friendship. So men and women come from the same planet after all."[1]

When I was first married, there was not an abundance of marriage books on the market. However, one favorite, *A Severe Mercy* by Sheldon Vanauken, made a lasting impression on my heart. It was an autobiography about the love between Sheldon and his wife, Davy. It wasn't meant to be an instructional book, but it held many treasures that impacted my marriage and my life.

In its pages, Vanauken shared one of the key elements of his and Davy's profound love:

> "Look," we said, "what is it that draws two people into closeness and love? Of course there's the mystery of physical attraction, but beyond that it's the things they share. We both love strawberries and ships and collies and poems and all beauty, and all those things bind us together. Those sharings just happened to be; but what we must do now is share everything. If one of us likes anything, there must be something to like in it—and the other one must find it—every single thing that either of us likes. That way we shall create a thousand strands, great and small, that will link us together. Then we shall be so close that it would be impossible—unthinkable—for either of us to suppose that we could ever recreate such closeness with anyone else. And our trust in each other will not only be based on love and loyalty, but on the fact of a thousand sharings—a thousand strands twisted into something unbreakable."[2]

Vanauken beautifully described the unbreakable bond that exists between intimate lovers and friends. In another book, he warned of creeping separateness that can threaten that oneness.

> There is such a thing as creeping separateness. What do young people who are freshly married do? They can't rest when they're apart. They want to be together all the time. But they develop separate interests, especially if they have separate jobs and some separate friends. So they drift apart. Pretty soon they have little in common except, maybe, the

children. So the stage is set for one of them to fall in love with someone else. Later they'll say the reason for the divorce was that he/she fell in love with someone else, but it wasn't that at all. It was because they let themselves grow apart.[3]

Let's take a look at ways to create those "thousand strands twisted into something unbreakable" so that creeping separateness doesn't have a chance to occur.

SIXTEEN

Creating Commonalities

When love is new, it seems couples want to spend every waking hour forming those "strands of a thousand sharings." Why, even changing the oil in the car becomes an exciting activity when they're doing it together. During the dating days, Miss Shop-Till-I-Drop suddenly loves watching NFL football on TV and Mr. Macho takes a sudden interest in time at the mall...as long as they are together. But what happens after the "I do's"?

I believe that continuing to form those strands of a thousand sharings becomes even more important as the mundane days of everyday living set in. The more intertwined the lives, the stronger the cord will be. Let's look at three areas where we can create commalities: his work, his play, and his world.

His Work

I daresay that a large percent of affairs begin in the workplace where a man and a woman work together for common goals, share common stresses, and celebrate common victories. All too often a man comes home from work to a wife who has no idea how he spent his day.

As I mentioned earlier, my husband is a dentist and I have a degree in dental hygiene. I helped him build his practice and understand the stresses of working in itty-bitty mouths all day long. I can sympathize with the struggles of getting the porcelain margin of a veneer on the facial of number eight just right. I understand the frustrations of having the occlusion of a five-unit bridge too high. (You don't know what I'm talking about? That's my point! We do.)

I know it is rare for husbands and wives to share the same profession, and most of the time counselors discourage couples from working together. But I believe the wife of your man's dreams enters his world and takes an interest in what he does at work, not just the paycheck he brings home at the end of the week.

Is your husband a stockbroker? Then learn to read those little numbers in the *Wall Street Journal*. Is your husband a banker? Then learn about IRAs, mutual funds, and compound interest. Is your husband a builder? Go to construction sites and watch his progress. Learn about Sheetrock quality or why a 2 x 4 is really a 1½ x 3½.

When your husband comes home from work, ask him about what happened during the day (or night)…and then actively listen. (We'll get to ways to be an active listener later in the chapter.) Also, ask him how you can pray for him each morning before he leaves for work. You may not be able to hold the nail for him, but praying for him during the day may ensure that he will hit the nail on the head every time.

His Play

Licensed clinical psychologist and marriage therapist Dr. Willard Harley notes in *His Needs, Her Needs* that one of man's five greatest needs in a wife is recreational companionship.[1] That means that your man wants to have a good time with you. He wants you to share his outside interests. He wants to laugh with you, play with you, and enjoy your company.

It is not uncommon for a woman to enter a man's recreational world when the couple is dating. She seemingly enjoys riding bikes, attending basketball games, and watching football on TV. However, once she "reels in the big fish," she often hangs up the pole. After marriage, women tend to try to get husbands more interested in their activities, such as visiting a flea market, attending the opera, or, dare I say, going shopping. "I don't really want to go hunting this weekend," she says. "Why don't you get some guys together and go without me?" This causes the poor guy to wonder what happened to the gal who was eager to rise before daybreak, dress in camouflage, and sit in the woods for hours looking for quail.

TV commercials show back-slapping men around the campfire, cooking clams and drinking their favorite brew. "It doesn't get any better than this," the announcer says. But studies show that it does get better than that. Men love spending recreational time with their wives.

When Steve and I were dating and newly married, he played on city league softball and basketball teams. I cannot do anything that involves a ball, but I could be at the games to cheer him on. The first winter of our relationship, I took Steve up to the mountains and taught him how to snow ski. I had been skiing for several years and he was eager to learn a new sport. Today, 20-plus years later, we still enjoy snow skiing as a family.

Author Leil Lowndes wrote, "A man wants a woman who enjoys the same activities, one he can have fun with. He likes to feel they can play tennis, go to concerts or basketball games or movies, or just sit at home and be side-by-side couch potatoes. Doing things together is important to a woman too, but it's higher on the male wish list."[2]

A husband and a wife can't share every actitivy. Steve took one look at my golf swing and said, "Honey, why don't we take some ballroom dance classes, and you leave the golf to me?"

> *My wife is a classic choleric: work, work, work. I am a classic sanguine: play, play, play. She resents my downtime, especially spent watching college football*

and basketball. She doesn't nag me anymore, but she lets me know in subtle ways that she resents it. —William

My wife joyfully shares in some of my hobbies, and she doesn't become irritated when I do hobby stuff without her. For example, she doesn't ridicule me or make me feel guilty for going hunting with my friends. —Nathan

The woman of my dreams is a companion in friendship and activities. She makes home a harmonious place to be. —Adam

I remember sitting in English class with a fellow cheerleader in the eleventh grade. The teacher looked up at my friend dressed in her spiffy cheerleader outfit and said, "Belinda, I bet you don't even know what a gridiron is. What is it?"

Sheepishly she replied, "Is it something you cook pancakes on?"

The boys in the class just howled! Oh, how frustrated the team would be as we cheered "take it away," when in fact we had the ball. Or as we yelled, "get the ball back" when our offensive team was working the ball down the field as hard as they could.

While we may not be able to join our husbands in certain sports, we can learn about the ins and outs of the game and show interest. Does your husband like football? Learn what a tight end does and why the official keeps throwing those handkerchiefs in the air. Does he play golf? Learn why a birdie is better than a bogey and ask him what he shot when he returns home from a round on the greens. Does he like to hunt? Learn how to cook venison or quail.

While you may have different recreational interests, I suggest you make a list of activities and discover a few that you can do together. On the next page is a list of activities to consider:

acrobatics, acting, aerobics, antique collecting, archery, art collecting, auto customizing, badminton, ballet, baseball, bicycling, board games, boating, bobsledding, bowling, boxing, bridge, camping, canoeing, checkers, chess, computer programming, concerts, cooking, cricket, croquet, crossword puzzles, curling, dancing, debating, deck tennis, decorating, dining out, diving, drawing, engraving, fencing, field events, fishing, football, gardening, golf, handball, hiking, hockey, horseback riding, horseshoe pitching, hunting, ice-skating, jogging, judo, karate, kayaking, knitting, model building, mountain climbing, movie going, needlework, opera, painting, poetry, polo, puzzles, quilting, racquetball, rafting, reading, rowing, sailing, sewing, shooting, singing, skiing, skin diving, table tennis, tennis, traveling, volleyball, walking, weightlifting, windsurfing, yachting[3]

I wish my wife understood my need and desire for her companionship in activities I enjoy. —Terry

My wife is really good at taking an interest in what interests me—like sports. —Carter

One thing I wish my wife understood is that I feel her relationship with God is the most important thing. Also, it is a lot easier to go the extra mile for what is most important to her when our sexual relationship is healthy. —Sean

I long to spend more time with my wife and wish she felt the same about me. —Jeremy

His World

Al Janssen grew up in New York City, and as a young boy his greatest dream was to play major league baseball in Yankee Stadium. His ability did not match his dream, so he did the next best thing to playing the game—he became a sports writer. After college, Al landed his first book contract to write about a defensive tackle for the Green Bay Packers. That Thanksgiving week he observed team practices, visited the Packers' Hall of Fame, and had a pass for Lambeau Field that allowed him access anywhere in the stadium during the Packers' game against their archrivals, the Chicago Bears. His twenty-seventh birthday also occurred that week, and he couldn't imagine a better way to celebrate it.

With all this excitement, Al was puzzled as to why he wasn't happy. One reason, he decided, was that it was the coldest day ever for an NFL game. Since he lived in Arizona, he was unprepared for the below-zero windchill as he roamed the sidelines. But there was another chill that froze his heart...he had no one with whom to share his experience.

"As I thawed out in the motel that night," he explained, "I was acutely aware of an intense loneliness. I had many friends. But I longed for someone to phone who was expecting my call, to whom I could relate all my experiences and hear on the other end that she was excited with me. I needed to know someone loved me and missed me and wanted to tell me all about what was happening in her life. Was there one person in this world who would care more about me than anyone else? Was there a single individual with whom I could share my dreams and my journey?"[4]

That night in his hotel room, Al asked God to send him a wife. He prayed for someone who would be his closest friend, someone with whom he could share his life. Five months later, God answered Al's prayer and sent him Jo Ann.

I believe God has placed in each human heart the desire to know and be known. We long for intimacy, even as children. Little girls want a best friend with whom they can share secrets, hold hands, and write love notes. Little boys want a blood brother with whom they can make a secret pact, have a secret handshake, and play catch. While we may have glimpses of intimate friendship throughout our lives, it is only through the marriage relationship, wherein a man and a woman become one flesh, that true intimacy can be realized.

Unfortunately, this kind of intimacy is difficult to achieve. As with any close friendship, there is the fear "if he or she really knew me, they may not like me." Intimate friendship goes beyond that fear. A true friend is one that knows all your faults and loves you anyway.

There is no way you are going to share everything with your husband—and you shouldn't. He will have some interests that are solely his and you will have some interests that are solely yours. I don't expect Steve to take up sewing, and he doesn't expect me to read *Sports Illustrated* cover to cover. But we can both show an interest in what the other is interested in.

For example, Steve collects baseball cards. Honestly, I don't understand the excitement of putting those cards in books, rating them on their condition, and gathering with other collectors to compare their treasures. However, for one of his birthday surprises, I researched and found a large baseball card show in Philadelphia, booked him a flight, rented him a car, reserved him a hotel room, and *voilà*—gave him one of the best birthday gifts ever. I entered his world.

One summer the ministry where I work was in a very dry time financially. Even though Steve supported the ministry financially, he decided he wanted to do more to help us get out of the slump. Steve sold one of his prized baseball cards and helped us meet our financial obligations. He entered my world.

The woman of my dreams is one who creates a haven of peace and love that draws me home like a magnet, where it is always safe to bare my soul, in trouble or in joy. —Tom

The woman of my dreams is someone who takes joy in figuring out the puzzle of who I am. Someone who recognizes that, all day long, I am expected to have all the answers and quietly understands that I don't. A woman who deeply enjoys simple things, like a sunset, the power of the unexpected, a mountain, and a memory. —Pete

I want my wife to explore with me, learn with me, and be my closest confidante. —Jeff

As we have already seen, the word "helper" in Genesis 2:18 can be translated "rescuer." What exactly did Eve "rescue" Adam from? Perhaps it was loneliness. God had said, "It is not good for man to be alone."

Before the industrial age, it came naturally for a husband and wife to work together for common goals. Their very existence depended on it. My paternal grandparents ran a general store during the Depression. My maternal grandparents ran a farm with the help of their 12 children. I doubt they ever sat down and mapped out their hopes and dreams, but rather lived from day to day to put food on the table and clothes on their backs.

But we've come a long way from the agricultural age, and husbands and wives are often going in a hundred different directions. If we want to become truly one, we must be intentional in sharing work and play. We must share a life. As I've often said, "In our house, there are no 'his' and 'her' towels. We are living out one life in two bodies." Steve and I echo Sheldon Vanauken, "Our trust in each other will not only be based on love and loyalty, but on the fact of a thousand sharings—a thousand strands twisted into something unbreakable."

Man's Best Friend

Have you ever thought about why the dog is called "man's best friend"? For 13 years we had a golden retriever named Ginger.

She and Steve had a special bond, and she always liked him best. Ginger was loyal, didn't nag, and loved him no matter how much attention he paid to her on any given day. When she heard his car rounding the corner in the evening, Ginger jumped up from a dead slumber and began to run around in circles from mere excitement. When he opened the car door, she ran over to Steve, laid her head on his leg, and wagged her tail with all the force of a motorized metronome. Often, at the mere sight of Steve, Ginger rolled over on her back, beckoning him to rub her tummy. She always responded to his touch as though it were heaven on earth. Okay, girls, are we getting the picture here?

SEVENTEEN

Communicating Effectively

Do you remember those first days with the man who became your husband? You wanted to know everything there was to know about him: what his family members were like, his favorite food, his favorite subject in school, what he wanted in a wife, how many children he wanted, his favorite color, etc. You studied him as though you were preparing for a final exam. Now that you're married, you've only just begun to unlock the heart of your man.

Talking is something that just comes natural to us girls. Research makes it clear that little girls are more verbal than little boys. Dr. James Dobson notes: "God may have given her (the wife) fifty thousand words per day and her husband only twenty-five thousand. He comes home from work with 24,975 used up and merely grunts his way through the evening. He may descend into Monday-night football while his wife is dying to expend her remaining twenty-five thousand words. That means, when your husband comes home from work, he most likely is running low in the words department."[1]

When it comes to understanding how a man's mind works in the words department, reading the newspaper is an effective exercise. A trained newspaper reporter will give the article a catchy title, and then he or she will list the important facts of the article in the first few sentences. If you are intrigued, you'll read more. If not, you've obtained the gist of the situation in the first paragraph and that may be enough. Bingo. That's how the male mind wants to receive information. First get his attention. (During the middle of changing the oil in the car or during the last two minutes of an NFL playoff game might not be the best time to expect his full attention.) Give him a title. ("I need to talk to you about our son's wrecking the car last night.") Give him the main points. ("He drove your car, exceeded the speed limit by 20 miles per hour, and hit a fence.") Then, move along to the other paragraphs of interest, such as ramifications and emotions. ("I am furious and think we should take the keys away from him for a month, make him pay for the damages, and insist he take a driver's safety class for the next four Saturdays.")

While these are good pointers for everyday conversation, intimate communication happens on a much deeper level. A man who may not enjoy chitchat still longs for intimate communication with the woman of his dreams. If she's smart, she'll watch out for those rare invitations and RSVP with all the homing devices God has given her.

Many men hear echoes from childhood that falsely taunt, "Big boys don't cry." They recall teasing jabs of being called a "mama's boy," "wuss," or "sissy" when they showed signs of weakness or, heaven forbid, a tear. Very early in life, boys learn to hide their hurt under layers and layers of false manliness. Like gearing up with shoulder pads, helmets, and knee pads, men wear protective coverings to prevent their emotions from being injured in the game of life. Only through the unconditional and accepting love of the woman of his dreams will he begin to shed the protective shield over his heart and expose the tenderness therein.

Have you noticed how God puts some of the most beautiful and precious treasures in rough and rugged exteriors? Inside a rough and craggy oyster shell lies the beautiful pearl, underneath the brown tough skin of a kiwi is a vibrant delicious fruit, and in the dark recesses of a coal mine are buried valuable diamonds.

While your man may appear to be rough and tough on the outside, just below the surface is a treasure.

> *I wish my wife understood that I grew up on Mars, not Venus, and that when I say something there is no hidden message. We're not that smart on Mars.* —Travis

> *I wish my wife understood my need to be able to say what I feel without the fear of her getting upset.* —Rich

> *My wife understands that I need quiet time at the end of the day to unwind.* —Tom

Intimate Communication

In my book *Being a Great Mom, Raising Great Kids*, I go into detail about the importance of listening to your child. Along the same lines, the woman of your man's dreams is one who listens not just with her ears, but with her whole being. Let's take a look at how to listen.

We listen with our eyes. How do you feel when you are trying to have a conversation with someone and they are not making eye contact? How do I feel when my husband is watching a football game and I walk into the room to tell him something? It is not enough for him to push the mute button. I want him to turn his handsome head, make eye contact, and pay attention. I mean, who's more important, the Carolina Panthers or *moi*? (It may be the Panthers. We'll get to that in a moment.) One way we show our husband we love him is by stopping what we are doing and turning to face him when he speaks. This shows him that we are tuned in and what he has to say is important to us.

When I was on the safety patrol in the sixth grade, we learned the axiom: Stop—Look—Listen before allowing our fellow students to cross the street. Those same three words are a good rule of thumb to follow when listening as well. Stop what you're doing. Look your man in the eye. Listen to what he has to say. Now you're safe to go!

> *I am convinced that my wife, more than any other person on earth, has a thorough awareness and understanding of me and my needs.* —*Russ*

> *Our greatest struggle has been open communication. My wife came from a home where people did not express what they were feeling. I think the best way to alleviate that has been to just talk about everything and allow our feelings to come out.* —*Will*

> *The woman of my dreams likes to talk with me and listen to me.* —*Joseph*

We listen with our ears. This may seem redundant, but far too many times we nod and agree but let the flow of words go in one ear and out the other. I was struck by an article in the *Charlotte Observer* about a friend for hire. A woman was described as a "friend for hire," earning as much as $500 a month to sit and listen to whatever a person wanted to talk about. She is called a "personal development coach," someone who helps people focus and make decisions. Basically, she receives payment for two things: asking good questions and telling the truth. The *Observer* noted that *Newsweek* referred to this type of coaching as "part consultant, part motivational speaker, part therapist and part rent-a-friend."[2]

A startling Kansas newspaper ad read: "I will listen to you, without comment, for thirty minutes for $5."[3] The person who placed the ad received 10 to 20 calls per day. The man in your life wants a companion who will truly listen to what he has to say. Let's make sure he doesn't have to "hire a friend" or phone a stranger, but has the ear of the woman of his dreams—you.

> *The woman of my dreams is a good listener and cares about what I think.* —*Josh*

> *My wife is exceptional about understanding me and even helps me understand myself better!* —*Herb*

> *Sometimes I think my wife understands me better than I understand myself. She listens and tries to understand. Most importantly, she desires to know me better—I am so blessed.* —*Bill*

We listen with our facial expressions. Charles Swindoll tells a story reported by Dr. Karl Menninger about how facial expressions invite someone in or shut them out.

> During his days as president, Thomas Jefferson and a group of companions were traveling across the country on horseback. They came to a river that had left its banks because of a recent downpour. The swollen river had washed the bridge away. Each rider was forced to ford the river on horseback, fighting for his life against the rapid currents. The very real possibility of death threatened each rider, which caused a traveler who was not part of their group to step aside and watch. After several had plunged in and made it to the other side, the stranger asked President Jefferson if he would ferry him across the river. The president agreed without hesitation. The man climbed on, and shortly thereafter the two of

them made it safely to the other side. As the stranger slid off the back of the saddle onto dry ground, one in the group asked him, "Tell me, why did you select the president to ask this favor of?" The man was shocked, admitting he had no idea it was the president who had helped him. "All I know," he said, "is that on some of your faces was written the answer 'No,' and on some of them was the answer 'Yes.' His was a 'Yes' face."[4]

When my husband comes to me, do I have a "yes" face that says, "I'm interested in what you have to say. I want to help you in any way I can. You are the most important person in my day"? Or do I have a "no" face that says, "What do you want now? Can't you see I'm busy? What I am doing is much more important than any of your trivial concerns"?

The woman of his dreams initiates intimate friendship, has a "yes" face, and doesn't force her husband to look for that welcoming look anywhere beyond his own front door.

We listen with our lips. Now maybe you thought the whole idea of listening was to keep the lips zipped. However, one of the most effective ways to show that we are truly listening is to *complete the loop* in the conversation by asking follow-up questions or making comments to show we're engaged. For example, if your husband comes home from work and says, "I had a terrible day at work," then you would complete the loop by responding, "Really? Tell me what happened."

Such a comment will show him you care and are interested in what happened during his day.

Here's another example:

> Husband: "I had to confront Bob at work today. He's just plain lazy."
>
> Wife: "Really? What happened? How did you handle it?"

As your husband begins to share the details of his day, asking questions shows that you are interested and in touch with what he's experiencing. If his comments are met by silence or a sharp detour of you telling him what went on in your day, he will think you don't care about what is going on in his life and will very likely withdraw or find someone else who will listen.

Along with silence, judgmental comments will also kill a conversation. Let's go back to the previous scenario.

> Husband: "I had to confront Bob at work today. He's just plain lazy."

> Wife: "I don't think Bob's lazy. He's just having a hard time. I think you're too hard on him."

Whoa. That wife has just done one of two things: She's thrown cold water on that conversation and it will come to an abrupt stop or she's made her husband angry and he wishes he'd kept his thoughts to himself. Either way, silence or judging will end a conversation, but asking questions will draw him out and invite him to tell you more.

> *I wish my wife understood that communication is as important to me as it is to her. As a man, I deal in specifics and am more compartmentalized. I am horrible at mind reading.* —Craig.

> *One of our biggest struggles has been communication. I tend to hold things in for two reasons: I don't want to bother her as she has enough on her plate, and when I do communicate, the response seems to be negative or I get a lot of advice when all I want is an ear.* —Paul

> *One thing I wish my wife understood better about me is my desire to have her listen to me—really listen,*

not only with her ears, but also with her mind. I want her to understand me when I talk and explain things to her. I want her to work with me, not against me— to be my partner, not my antagonist. I want her support and cooperation—and not a challenge. —Bob

We listen with our mind. As you can see, listening is not passive but very active. A good listener is trained to use every homing device God has provided: eyes, ears, facial expressions, lips, and mind. One of the best ways to cultivate conversation with your husband is to ask good questions. Notice I said *good* questions.

There are two types of questions to choose from: closed and open. A closed question is one that can be answered with one word: "good," "bad," "okay," "yes," "no." For example, "Did you have a good day at work?" is a closed question. "What happened at your sales meeting today?" is an open question. An open question is one that draws out the person and requires a more thoughtful answer. Once your husband begins to answer such questions, complete the loop by asking follow-up questions. As soon as you begin to give unsolicited advice or judge his actions, the wall will go up and the opportunity to initiate intimate friendship through listening will slip away.

Here are 25 great questions to initiate conversation. Remember, timing is everything. These are questions that beg discussion, so don't ask them during the football game, when he's winding down after an exhausting day at the office, or while he's reading the paper. The questions are endless! Let these few spark questions of your own!

1. What do you think heaven looks like?
2. What was your favorite thing to do as a child?
3. Who was the biggest bully in your neighborhood when you were growing up?
4. What is the most scared you have ever been in your life?

5. If you were going to spend one year in the desert and could take along three things from the bedroom, what would they be?

6. What is your best Christmas memory?

7. What is the nicest thing I ever did for you?

8. If you could be a cartoon character, who would you be?

9. If you could be a superhero, who would you be?

10. When you pray, how do you see God?

11. If you could be an animal for the day, what would you be? Why?

12. What were you most afraid of as a child?

13. What is your greatest fear now?

14. Who is your hero?

15. What are your top five favorite movies?

16. When you get to heaven, other than God and Jesus, whom do you want to spend time talking to?

17. What one question would you like for God to answer?

18. Who was the first girl you kissed and how old were you?

19. What would your fantasy vacation be like?

20. What is your idea of a perfect day?

21. If you could have three cars for three different moods, what would they be?

22. What person in history would you like to visit?

23. If you could be a professional sports player, what team would you play for and what position would you play?

24. Where have you always wanted to go but have never gone?

25. What have you always wanted to do but have never done?

The woman of my dreams is loving, caring, and forgiving. —Jim

My wife is my perfect mate. Her radiance and commitment overwhelms me as if we just had our first date. We've been together for 31 years. —Kevin

The wife of my dreams is my best friend. —Greg

Friendship and respect are top priorities for me. —Gary

We listen with our heart. Finally, the woman of your man's dreams listens with her heart. She listens to the feelings as well as the facts. She uses her intuition as she processes the information. What lies in the heart of a man is like treasure in deep waters, but a wise woman will draw him out (Proverbs 20:5). A man wants to communicate with the woman of his dreams on an intimate level. The more we listen with our hearts, the more they will speak from their hearts. In order for this level of communication to take place, a man must feel completely safe, trusting that you would never divulge a confidence or share his heart with anyone else. If he does not have that assurance, you most likely will not have the honor of engaging in the deepest level of intimate friendship. When a man feels he can share his heart without betrayal, judgment, or condemnation, he will take the woman of his dreams to new depths of his soul that many leave unexplored.

Years ago, I went snorkeling in the Caribbean for the first time. All my life I had been around water—bobbing up and down in boats on the ocean, skimming across the surface of lakes, and canoeing down the narrow Tar River in my hometown. Occasionally I'd catch a glimpse of fish scurrying though the currents or be entertained by a porpoise or dolphin arching above the waves. However, when I put on goggles and learned to look below the surface, I discovered a whole new world. There were sea creatures dressed in vibrant yellow, royal blue, and exotic orange patterns. Gaily colored four-eyed butterfly fish, rainbow-striped parrot fish, buck-teeth porcupine fish, and minnow-like zebra fish frolicked about in arm's reach. New playmates peeked in and out of the coral reef, teasingly nipped at my toes, and flirted with my goggles.

Amazingly, all that beauty existed just below the surface of the water, but I would never have seen it had I not been willing to dive in. The swaying anemone, the craggy coral, the percolating jellyfish, the feathery finned angelfish—all uniquely created and a visual wonder. Likewise, your husband, and my husband, are magnificent creatures! The further we delve into their lives by initiating intimate friendship, the more we will appreciate their uniqueness. We have a choice as to whether we will stay on the surface or don the proper gear and dive deeper into their souls to discover hidden wonders lying just below. Surprises await us each new day—if we dare to dive in and keep exploring.

Each Christmas season my husband takes his staff and their husbands out to dinner. Last year, I sat next to Sherri's husband, Gene. I have known Gene for more than ten years, and I enjoyed our annual visit. On this particular visit, I decided to dive in a little deeper and explore Gene's heart.

"Gene, how's your work as the administrator of the assisted living center going?"

"It's going well," he answered. "I really enjoy getting to know the older folks."

"What's one of the best experiences you've had while working there?"

"Well, there have been so many. I can tell you about one situation with a man named Mr. Matthews. He had lots of ailments that needed to be monitored, but was just a delightful man. His first wife had passed away and his second wife was seriously ill and in a nursing home some miles away. Mr. Matthews always had a smile on his face and a song in his heart. Not only did he have a song in his heart, he had one in each of his pockets. See, Mr.

Matthews played the harmonica and had several instruments. In one pocket he had a harmonica that was tuned to C. In another, he had one tuned to D minor. He was amazing. He could play any tune you could name. He had been a minister in his younger days and was especially good at hymns."

As Gene talked about Mr. Matthews, his whole face lit up. I decided to dive deeper. "Did he have children," I asked.

"Mr. Matthews' stepchildren never gave him the time of day. I don't think they ever came to see him. One day, one of the kids called and said, 'Could you please tell Mr. Matthews that his wife just died?'

"I was stunned. Why didn't they tell him? How was I going to tell him this kind of news?

"So I walked into the recreation room, placed my hand on his shoulder, and said, 'Mr. Matthews, I don't know how to tell you this, but I just got a call that your wife has passed away.'

"The old man said, 'Well, I've told people to have faith all my life. Now it's time that I tell myself the same thing.' We both just sat there and cried.

"A few days later, I went to the funeral and sat with Mr. Matthews in a tent by the graveside. There were no other family members around. He said, 'Gene, you'll never know how much this means to me. I'll never forget you.'

"Several weeks later, one day when I was driving up to the assisted living center, he called me over to his chair and said again, 'Gene, I will never forget.'"

Gene went on to tell me more stories about his loving care of the elderly people in the assisted living center. With each story he told, there was a tenderness that was evidenced by the welling up of tears. Throughout the conversation, both of us teared up several times.

I had known Gene for many years, but on this evening I asked questions that invited him to share the depths of his heart with me. It was truly the main course of my meal.

As Steve and I drove home, I was once again reminded of the treasures that are hidden in the heart of a man. "A man's heart is a precious and private thing. A man is less likely than a woman to bare his soul or communicate every thought. His heart is often locked up and protected, a great treasure stored in a secure vault. The inner wealth represents the core of a man's whole being, the hub of all his activity, his identity as a man."[5] As a wife, you hold the key to your husband's heart, or at least you could. From the surveys I received, many men still cling to the key and keep the treasure stored away for fear their wives will squander the treasure or belittle what they hold dear.

The woman of his dreams is one who is interested enough to ask good questions, listen with her whole being, and provide a safe place for him to expose the hidden treasures within. After all, that's what friends are for.

> *Though we have been blessed to avoid major, marriage-threatening struggles, we have wrestled with communication. I have had to learn that she doesn't want me to necessarily solve every problem right then and there; she just wants me to listen to her. And she has a way of verbally stabbing me with a dagger, and then twisting it! Although after 19 years of marriage, she has mellowed considerably. Also, she used to say, "You thought..." or "You meant..." I despise having thoughts or motives ascribed to me that are not mine. Again, she rarely goes there because she has learned it's my hot button. Also, I have learned to communicate better. She needs that on a daily basis. I don't think it is a natural thing for me to do, but when I force myself to sit down and talk with her when I get home, she begins to glow, and I find myself enjoying it. —Winston*

It seems when we are discussing something that needs a decision, she will give a certain amount of information that favors a particular decision be made. When we decide, she brings out more information that requires a different decision be made. I wish she would give all pertinent information at the same time. If the issue deals with her and her responsibilities, make the decision and just let me know what the plan is. —Randy

Twenty-Five Ways to Be a Good Listener

1. Be patient.
2. Don't complete his sentences.
3. Let him finish, even if he seems to be rambling.
4. Don't interrupt.
5. Face your husband and make eye contact.
6. Lean forward, if you are seated, to show you are interested.
7. Stop what you are doing.
8. Ask good questions and avoid the word "why."
9. Ask his opinion about something that happened to you.
10. Ask him for his advice on a decision you have to make.
11. Don't jump to conclusions.
12. Don't give unsolicited advice.
13. Don't change the subject until he is finished with a subject.
14. Make verbal responses such as, "I see," "Really," "Uh-huh," to show you're paying attention.
15. Turn off the TV.
16. Put down the dishcloth, book, hairbrush, etc.

17. Encourage him to tell you more. "What else did he say?" "What did she do next?"
18. When he is telling of a struggle, rephrase and repeat what you heard. "What I hear you saying is that you felt your boss was being unfair when he asked you to take on three more clients with no extra compensation."
19. Let the telephone ring if he is in the middle of telling you something.
20. Don't glance at your watch or cross your arms.
21. Don't ask him to hurry.
22. If a child interrupts, tell him or her to wait until daddy is finished talking.
23. Don't tell him how he should have handled the situation differently.
24. Don't act bored.
25. Thank him for sharing with you.

Section Five

Safeguards Her Marriage

EIGHTEEN

In-Laws or Out-Laws?

Brian was 35 years old when he met Leigh Ann. All through undergraduate school, medical school, and pediatric residency, he had dated many young women, but he had not found the woman of his dreams. When he met Leigh Ann, he instantly fell in love with this 25-year-old beauty. She had everything he longed for in a wife: a sincere faith in Christ, a strong commitment to family, and a beauty that was unmatched. The icing on the cake was that she was crazy in love with him.

Brian's own family was riddled with divorce—much higher than the national average. He had watched the agony of many of his high school and college friends as they struggled through separation and divorce. "I feared divorce more than death," Brian shared with me.

So he waited until he was absolutely sure he had found the right woman before he took the plunge and signed on the dotted line with a permanent marker. In the genesis of their relationship, Leigh Ann showed great interest in Brian's friends, family, work, and hobbies. She was encouraging, sexually attentive, romantic, and the focus of Brian's life. However, there was one obstacle that prevented Brian and Leigh Ann from truly becoming "one." She refused to break the strong ties with her family and form a cord of three strands with her new husband and God. Here's a bit of Brian's story as he related it to me:

> I had always wanted a wife who had a strong commitment to family. When we were dating, I was attracted to the close relationship I observed between Leigh Ann and her parents and sisters. It never occurred to me that she would refuse to put our relationship above her relationship with her parents. It wasn't until our first Christmas as man and wife that I caught a glimpse of what the future held.
>
> Leigh Ann woke me up at the crack of dawn on Christmas morning. I groggily crawled out of bed and asked her why the rush. She wanted to get to her parents' house early! Early we did. We got there before anyone was even up. As we went through the day, I saw her happy, cheerful, and excited—much more so than she ever was when it was just the two of us. It was then I began to sense that Leigh Ann really wanted to be that little girl waking up with Mom and Dad on Christmas morning instead of celebrating her day (or her life) with me. From that day, and the many days that followed, I felt that my duty was to assimilate into her family instead of she and I forming a new family of our own.
>
> The dependency on her mother continued to grow like kudzu, strangling the very life from our marriage. They talked on the telephone several times a day, every day. There was not a decision to be made that did not have to have her mom's stamp of approval. Very rarely did my opinion count, and sometimes I was not consulted at all.
>
> You have to remember, I was a doctor who made life-and-death decisions all day long, and yet in my own home my opinions were ignored. Her family

traditions became our family traditions. Her family vacations became our family vacations. Her parents' decor became the pattern for our family decor.

I longed to be the spiritual leader of our home, but even that was sabotaged by Leigh Ann's dependence on her family. Since I was older and well established, I was an elder at my church and very involved. However, Leigh Ann insisted that we attend her parents' church when my term for elder was complete. I complied. When her parents changed churches, we followed them along.

I don't want you to get the idea that Brian was a complacent husband who said, "Yes, dear. Whatever you want, dear." For six years, he fought for their marriage and the biblical model of what a husband and wife should be. But because he loved his wife, he conceded to many requests that went against his better judgment. In a matter of six years, this man who once overflowed with life was reduced to a mere trickle. Finally, with false accusations of control and verbal abuse, Leigh Ann filed for divorce. She realized that Brian could not be manipulated, as her own father had been. Divorce, and all that came with it, was her last act of control. I asked Brian how he felt during this time:

> I didn't feel like a man at all. I felt so controlled and manipulated. I know the Bible says that we are to "die to self," but I think that means in relationship to Christ. I was dying as a man just to keep peace in our home. And you know what? It didn't keep peace at all. We fought all the time. I felt that my only role in the relationship was to give her what her mother could not...a paycheck and children. That was all she needed me for. I loved Leigh Ann, but I realized she was never going to love me more than she loved her mother. I would never have first place in her heart.

Brian's greatest fear was realized. He and Leigh Ann divorced. It was a brutal process and nobody won. Unfortunately, their children suffered the most.

Second Only to God

So far, we've talked about how the woman of his dreams is a woman who prays for him, respects him, adores him, and initiates intimate friendship with him. Now let's turn our attention to an area that is very tender to our tough guy's heart. The woman of his dreams places her man number one above every other human relationship—above her parents, above their children, and above all others. She safeguards her marriage against forces that threaten to wedge their way between her and her husband, and she stands as a sentry to protect them against anything that would pry them apart.

> *The woman of my dreams prioritizes me as her primary mission. She sees this mission as her primary means of service to God and as a form of worshiping Him. She leaves and cleaves.* —John

> *My wife does a great job of putting her family first, only behind God.* —Robert

> *My wife is the woman of my dreams. She loves God first, me second, and shows me daily.* —John

> *The wife of my dreams lets me know, in a way I understand, that next to God I'm the most important person in her life.* —David

Making the Break

It was a beautiful winter day with a dusting of snow on the ground and ice glistening on the tree branches that seemed to bow in our honor. Steve and I were on our way from the

University of North Carolina at Chapel Hill to Charlotte, his hometown, to deliver some wonderful news. The sky was Carolina Blue (you have to see it to believe it), and the whole world shimmered from the ice deposited the night before. Nature wasn't the only thing sparkling in the sun that day. Steve and I both were absolutely beaming from ear to ear, bursting with love from every pore of our being. We made the three-hour trip to Charlotte anticipating congratulations and adulations.

"Mom, Dad, sit down," Steve requested. "Sharon and I have something to tell you."

"What, son?" they asked in unison.

"We're engaged. We're going to get married," Steve continued.

At this point, the rest of the day becomes a blur. But I do distinctly remember Steve's mother pressing her head into the back of the couch as if she were either going to faint or be sick. Steve's dad just looked at us as though we had told him we had decided to move to Antarctica and raise coffee beans.

I didn't know much, but I knew this was not going well.

The next few hours were spent with Steve trying to convince his parents that he knew what he was doing. Yes, he was still in school, albeit graduate school. No, we had not dated very long, but how long was long enough? (He had dated one gal eight years before we met.) Honestly, I have forgotten most of the conversation, but I have never forgotten the sick feeling in the pit of my stomach. Later that evening, Steve's mom hugged me with all the passion of someone embracing a cactus and said, "Welcome to the family."

That was almost 25 years ago, and much has changed since then. I love Steve's parents dearly and they love me. We have a wonderful relationship, but we had a rough-and-rocky start. I know that many couples aren't so fortunate. While we say "Let no man put asunder" on our wedding day, sometimes it is the couple's very own family members who are doing the "asundering."

Among the most common problems in marriages today, sex, money, and in-laws top the list. Mother-in-law jokes are plentiful, but in-law problems are no laughing matter. While there are not an abundant supply of verses in the Bible concerning extended family, there is one primary directive: "Therefore shall a man leave his father and his mother, and shall cleave unto his wife: and they shall be one flesh" (Genesis 2:24 KJV). I find it interesting that God gave this instruction before there was even a mother and father to leave. God sees past, present, and future all at once, and He knew the problems that would arise from the refusal of a man or woman to leave their parents and cleave only to their marriage partner.

Steve and I have always felt the number one priority in our family is our family. At first it was our family of two and then, after Steven was born, it was our family of three. At times this decision has left both sets of in-laws disappointed when we did not meet their expectations; however, it has kept our little family unified.

It is common for holidays to be the most stressful time of the year for many people. We discovered that firsthand on our first *not so merry* Christmas as husband and wife. We had a decision to make. Which family would we visit? We were still in college and it was quite a dilemma. Neither of us had been away from our families at Christmas in our 24-year lives. Of course, my parents expected their only little girl to come home for the holidays—I had never missed a Christmas before. Of course, Steve's parents expected Steve to be at their house for the holidays. He's a twin, and the boys are always together for the holidays. Besides, if Steve's sister could drive three days from Oklahoma with her husband and three children, the least we could do was drive three hours.

In an effort to make everyone happy, we decided to have breakfast with my family, hurriedly exchange gifts and give quick hugs, and then race to Steve's parents four hours away in time for dinner. So among the "Please don't rush off" and "We wish you had been here earlier," we pleased no one. Steve and I were exhausted, and neither family was completely satisfied.

To top it off, Steve's grandmother died and our two-year-old niece went into the hospital with meningitis. Steve, his parents, and siblings went to the funeral in the mountains, my sister-in-law (the wife of Steve's twin) and I stayed to take care of our niece and nephew, and Steve's sister's husband stayed in the hospital with our other niece. In effect, the *real* Jayneses left and the in-laws stayed behind. After that weekend Steve and I decided we would never again go through another family crisis not walking hand in hand. As of that Christmas, we made a decision to "leave and cleave" no matter what.

This decision has caused some anger and frustration on both sides of our families over the years. However, they rejoice in the strong love and commitment they see in our marriage. We have watched several friends struggle, some to the point of divorce, because of the refusal of one party to cleave to the marriage partner and separate from the parents. Brian's story is not that uncommon.

The woman of his dreams makes a decision that her relationship with her husband is second only to her relationship with God.

> *My wife is creative, industrious, and wise. She isn't fooled by worldly distractions that pull other women away from their husbands and children.*
> *—Nicolas*

> *The woman of my dreams loves me more than any other person.* *—Herb*

> *What had been our biggest struggle? Money and extended family members.* *—Brian*

> *I wish my wife would give me the same amount of quality time and attention she gives everybody else.*
> *—Dave*

Leave and Cleave

When it comes to extended family, several questions need to be addressed. How often do we visit? How long do we stay? How long do the in-laws stay when they come to visit? Where do we spend Christmas or Thanksgiving? Do we spend vacation time with extended family? How much do we tell extended family about our finances? Our marital struggles? Our parenting decisions?

Questions such as these can be difficult to agree upon, but it is important to reach an agreement before the problem is staring you in the face (or knocking on the door).

The most important point is to reach an agreement that you are both comfortable with and that will honor your spouse. Remember, the most important family unit God has ordained is you and your spouse.

God does call us to honor our fathers and mothers: "Honor your father and mother. Then you will live a long, full life in the land the LORD your God will give you" (Exodus 20:12 NLT). This is the only commandment with a promise of future blessing. Author Sandra Aldrich wrote, "Honoring does not mean letting them order you around, pry into your personal finances, tell your kids to get haircuts, or rearrange your cabinets each time they visit. It means honoring their position. Once the child becomes an adult, it's important that a new relationship be built—more 'friend to friend' than 'parent to child.' "[1]

Dr. James Dobson states in his book *Solid Answers*, "If either the husband or wife has not been fully emancipated from the parents, it is best not to live near them. Autonomy is difficult for some mothers and fathers to grant, and close proximity is built for trouble."[2]

Most in-law problems are an issue of who's in control. Common phrases, such as "Don't you love us anymore?" "Your sister comes to see me every week" "You are always welcome at our house, but I guess it just doesn't work both ways" "You never call" are meant to gain control by administering an ample dose of guilt. I suggest not swallowing it. You're a grown woman with allegiance to the leader of your home. Here's a favorite response that all travelers of guilt trips need to say: "I'm sorry you feel that way." Go ahead, practice it. Stand in front of the mirror and form the words. "I'm sorry you feel that way."

But what about if the in-law problems are on your husband's side of the family? This book is designed to shed some light on how to become the woman of his dreams, but I realize that many in-law problems are with mamas who refuse to let go of their boys. The same advice I'm giving for us gals applies to the guys. We need to know that we hold first place in *his* heart.

Here is something for us to remember. Some men have been manipulated by controlling mothers all their lives. When his new wife sees this happening, anger begins to boil. Now the poor guy has two problem females in his life! One suggestion is to talk to your husband about the situation and try and come up with solutions that alleviate the feeling of being caught between a rock and a hard place. Something as simple as a monthly lunch date with his mother may make all the difference in the world.

The main thing your husband needs to know is where he stands with you (just as you desire to know where you stand with him). He may be silently asking, *Do you love me more than your parents? Am I number one in your life? Do you trust me to take care of you?*

Perhaps you've had an in-law or a parent with the following perspective. A mother was asked about her son's new wife. "Oh, she's so lazy. She expects my son to help her with the dishes and to babysit and go grocery shopping with her. I just don't know how long he can keep that pace up."

The visitor shook her had. "I'm sorry to hear that. How's your daughter's marriage going?"

The mother smiled. "She has the most wonderful husband! He helps her with the dishes, and he's happy to babysit and goes grocery shopping with her. He is just wonderful. She's fortunate to have gotten such a good man."[3]

Parents always tend to err on the side of their own child. Elizabeth Stone said, "To make a decision to have a child is momentous. It is to decide forever to have your heart go walking around outside your body." When that heart walks down the aisle with the woman of his dreams, it can be hard for some moms to let go.

I think it is much more of a problem for women to "leave and cleave" than for men. I've often heard "A son is a son until he takes a wife. A daughter is a daughter for the rest of her life." Hmm. Neither the man nor the woman needs to stop being a son or daughter to their parents. We do, however, need to learn how to be first and foremost a husband and a wife.

Do your in-laws encourage you to build a godly home that will last a lifetime? Or are they out-laws who rob you of the oneness you committed to on your wedding day? Pray about it. Talk about it. And above all, enjoy the miracle of two becoming one and keeping your husband first, second only to God.

Brian's Story Continues

I want to take you back a moment to Brian and Leigh Ann's story. If you remember, Leigh Ann had great difficulty separating from her parents and honoring her husband as leader of the home. Amazingly, through all the pain, Brian loved Leigh Ann and prayed for reconciliation. As the weeks and months after the divorce crept by, he began to see a softening of her heart toward him, and she began to realize the treasure she had so easily tossed away. Eventually, Leigh Ann asked Brian if they could try again. After two years of being divorced, they remarried.

"It's still a struggle," Brian admitted. "But now she's at least willing to try. I love her more than my own life, and I have a dream that one day she will love me the same."

"Brian," I asked, "what is the one thing you'd want to tell women who will read this book?"

"That's easy," he replied. "Don't get married until you are ready to put that man above every other human relationship. He's got to be number one."

"But most of the women who read this book will already be married. What would you say to them?"

"Well, I'd remind them of what it does to the soul of a man when he doesn't have first place in his wife's heart. He feels like a zero, a business partner, a nobody. If there is a decision to be made and somebody has to lose, make sure it's not your husband. And keep in mind that the best present you can give your husband is the feeling that you desire him above all else."

Brian is a handsome, well-educated, successful person who appears to have everything a man could want. But his heart's cry is to have a godly wife who is crazy about him, puts him before all other earthly relationships, and loves, honors, and respects him as leader of the home. From what I can tell, his dream is on the way to coming true.

In-Law Survival Guide

One way to avoid a crisis of any kind is to be prepared. Let's look at some key ways to prepare your heart and home for extended family gatherings.

Have a plan. If you decide ahead of time that you are going to visit your parents once a month or once a quarter, then everyone knows what to expect. This will alleviate the "you never come to see us" routine. If your parents know you are going to call once a week, it will alleviate the "you never call" lament.

Take a walk. If you are spending extended time with in-laws and feel tensions beginning to rise, take a walk, run an errand, or simply go outside and water the plants. A bit of fresh air can give a new perspective.

Destroy the list. One of the most destructive in-law tendencies is to make a list of offenses and then air them when the family gathering is over. Try not to make a list of grievances and hurtful comments, and avoid having a play-by-play review session of offenses, irritating habits, or disagreeable comments.

Create a list. Look for the good qualities in your in-laws and be sure to acknowledge them. Perhaps it is that they raised an incredible son!

Let it roll. There are scores of jokes about the tension between mothers-in-law and sons-in-law, but studies show that the most difficult relationship is the one between the mother-in-law and her daughter-in-law. Betsy's mother-in-law asked, "How are Bill's allergies?" "He doesn't have allergies," Betsy replied. "I raised him and I know he has allergies!" the mom proclaimed. Just listen and then let comments roll off your back.

Prepare for holidays. Ask your husband how he would like to spend the holidays and consider alternating with traditions from your family.

Pray. Ask God to show you if you are seeking your parents' approval above that of your husband.

NINETEEN

Then There
Were Three

Do you remember the old childhood chant "First comes love, then comes marriage, then comes Susie with the baby carriage"? Did you ever wonder why there wasn't a second verse? I've watched what happens to couples after the babies start to come. Too many times a husband gets pushed out of his first-place position and has to resign himself to playing second fiddle. Obviously a child requires more time and energy than a grown man, but it is the skillful wife who reassures her guy that he is still number one in her heart.

Rob Parsons, author of the *60-Minute Marriage Builder,* wrote about the adjustment his marriage went through after the birth of their first child. "I have sympathy for the person who said, 'Insanity is hereditary—you get it from your kids!' I don't think I could love my children more, but why didn't anybody warn my wife and me of the changes they were going to cause in our relationship? One minute Diane and I were spending our evenings taking walks together, visiting friends, and reading in front of the fire. The next we were walking the halls at midnight singing nursery rhymes and dealing with postpartum depression—in me!"[1]

Parsons is a legal consultant and family advocate. A large part of his counseling is spent urging parents to spend time with their children; nevertheless, he warns that when one parent becomes obsessed with a child to the exclusion of the other parent, the marriage begins to operate as though there's an affair going on.[2]

In a majority of my surveys with men, they noted that the one thing their wife did well was "mother."

> *I wish my wife would show more support when it comes to guiding children through difficult times. When they rebel, I need her support more than ever, and, unfortunately, that's when her support ebbs. She needs to be part of the solution rather than part of the problem. She doesn't realize that her attitude and the way she speaks to me greatly affects the kids.* —Rick

> *What is one thing my wife does well? She cares for the children (sometimes too much).* —Matt

> *My wife is a wonderful mother, highly devoted to them and always seeking for their best.* —Eric

> *What is one thing my wife does well? She is a great mother.* —Joe Everyman (This was a response from a very large percentage of the questionnaire respondents.)

Dr. John Roseman noted: "Today's typical wife, as soon as she becomes a parent, begins to act as if she took a marriage vow that read, 'I take you to be my husband, until children do us part.'"[3]

I can remember a time, and not too long ago, when a wife who became a mother remained first and foremost a wife. A woman who worked outside the home was referred to as a "working wife," and a woman who worked in the home was referred to as a "housewife."

But a paradigm shift has occurred in our way of thinking that is reflected in the terms we use to describe a woman's employment status. Today's woman in the same circumstances is referred to as a "working mom" or a "stay-at-home mom." Now, some might think that is an improvement. After all, who wants to be married to her house? But I think the change is more of a reflection of the culture's shift of importance from being a wife to being a mother. Our focus has shifted from a home that is centered on the marriage unit to one that is centered on the children. That concerns me.

Roseman goes on to say: "This shift came about largely because America's shifted to a self-esteem based child-rearing philosophy, and women became persuaded that the mother who paid the most attention to and did the most for her child was the best mom of them all."[4]

Unfortunately, many times this has occurred at the expense of the marriage. The wife becomes engrossed in her children's lives, and the husband becomes engrossed in his career. Twenty years later, they look up from their cereal bowls and say, "Who are you?"

I believe the best mom of all is the one who loves her husband and gives her children the security of living within the protection of a rock-solid marriage, a marriage that exemplifies and models for them what God intended.

I remember when I was six years old, my heart's greatest desire was to have a mommy and daddy who loved each other. My parents had a tumultuous marriage. They fought both verbally and physically in my presence. I felt as though I lived on an earthquake fault line, never knowing when the big one was going to hit. There were many "big ones."

Once, when I had gone to visit my favorite aunt in Connecticut, she took me shopping to buy my mother a present. I picked out a very transparent pale yellow very lacy negligee. Everyone got a huge laugh out of my selection. But the truth was, in my little girl heart, I thought that if my mom was dressed in that nighty, then maybe my dad would like it. Then maybe my dad would like her. Then maybe she would like him. Then maybe everything would be okay.

A mother should never feel guilty for putting her husband before her children. Giving them the security of knowing that their parents love each other is one of the best gifts she can give them in the long run.

I wish my wife and I spent more time together without the kids. —Randy

The greatest struggle in our marriage has been arguments about the children. —Russ

I wish my wife understood my need to be her first priority, after Jesus and BEFORE the kids or other outside interests. —Craig

The woman of my dreams is the woman I'm married to right now. She is tenderhearted, caring, and soft-spoken (even though she's an attorney). She stays focused on our relationship. —Patrick

My wife and I have been married for more than 12 years. During this time we've had three children and have gone through periods where she worked outside the home or stayed with the children. For the entire period, she has not failed to wake up early in the morning to spend time with me and fix me breakfast before I go to work. This has meant a lot to me. —Travis

It has been said that "sex makes little kids and kids make little sex." Linda Dillow and Lorraine Pinuts, authors of *Intimate Issues,* note the following: "In one study, over six thousand couples were interviewed when they had no children and again five years later after they had become parents. The finding showed that after becoming parents, couples expressed a significant drop in marital satisfaction."[5] A more encouraging survey discussed in "The Transition to Parenthood" says that of 250 couples surveyed, 20 percent experienced notable improvement after having children.[6]

So one way or another, having children will affect your marriage. I hope you'll make a decision to be in that 20 percent that notices an improvement. How? By keeping daddy first. Don't let the new little man in your life dethrone the ruling king. And that little princess who stole your heart? Make sure she knows you're still the queen.

Keeping Daddy First

One of the best ways for keeping daddy first in your home is to have a plan. Let's look at several key ways to help your husband feel like the king of his castle regardless of how many little princes and princesses are vying for your attention.

Get away. Once or twice a year, get away for a night or weekend as a couple. My son was one year old when we left him for a weekend the first time. I missed him like crazy, but it did wonders for my husband to be the focus of all my attention for two days.

Get creative. Have a date night once a week. If money is a problem, trade babysitting with a friend. The date doesn't have to be expensive. Just a simple cup of coffee at a coffee shop or a walk around the park. The idea is to get alone and focus on each other. While there, try to keep the conversation away from the kids.

Get lovey-dovey. When your husband comes home from work, stop what you're doing and give him a big hug and kiss. If the kids are around to see it—all the better. Children need to see their parents show affection, and your greeting says to them, "I love this man and I'm glad he's home."

Get intentional. Be intentional about looking for ways to let your husband know that he's still number one in your book. Whether it's cooking a favorite meal or wearing a favorite night-gown, let him know you're still thinking of his desires.

Get personal. Have conversations that are not always focused on the children. A good place to start is with the questions in chapter 17 of this book.

Get involved. Get dad involved, that is. Think about how a mother is essential to a baby's survival. God gave us breasts so that the baby's very nourishment is dependent on our care. In order to help your husband feel needed, involve him in taking care of the baby. Share as many tasks as possible. By giving the baby a bottle, changing a diaper, or rocking him to sleep, your husband will feel as though he is needed and important in shared responsibilities.

Get practical. If your sex life takes a dip for a few months after the arrival of a new baby, make sure your husband knows it is not a sign of rejection but of exhaustion. Then think of some practical ways to reignite the flame.

Then There Were Two—Again

For the 18 years my son lived at home, Valentine's Day was a special day at our house. I served up a dinner of pink creamed potatoes, heart-shaped hamburgers, heart-shaped biscuits, red-velvet cupcakes with white icing, and pink lemonade. Red Mylar balloons danced from the kitchen chairs, and dinner was served on Valentine plates with red napkins. Of course, the entire meal was sprinkled with lots of love.

But something happened the year my son went off to college that caused a shift in this Jaynes family tradition. Somehow, pink-tinted creamed potatoes and heart-shaped hamburgers didn't hold the same magic, and 24 cupcakes seemed a bit much for just the two of us. As the day approached, Steve and I made a decision to start a new tradition—a romantic dinner out.

Because Valentine's Day fell on a Friday that year, Steve and I decided to celebrate on Thursday to avoid the crowds. I can safely say we avoided the crowds. When we arrived at the cozy candlelit restaurant, we were the only two customers there. Empty nest…empty house…empty restaurant.

"Boy, you know how to make a girl feel special," I teased Steve. "You reserved the entire restaurant for me!"

Of course it was only a fluke, but then again, I think God was giving us a special Valentine gift of our own. Throughout the entire evening, we had the place to ourselves. For several hours, waiters and waitresses gave their entire attention to one couple adjusting to a meal without pink creamed potatoes and red-velvet cupcakes. Steve and I held hands over a white tablecloth, looked into each other's eyes, and talked without worrying that the people at the next table would hear. Steve said a longer than usual blessing—and we had a wonderful time.

Thinking back on our first Valentine's Day as empty nesters, I am so grateful for our relationship. Sure, I missed the hubbub around my house, but we still had the day sprinkled with love. Through my ministry with women, I see so many couples who are investing most of their time and energy into raising their children. Schedules revolve around soccer practice, ball games, and school activities. Romance is placed on the back burner, and the marriage relationship is placed on hold for a more convenient time. Then one day, when the kids are gone, the couple rolls over in bed and realizes they are living with a stranger.

Don't get me wrong. I love being a mother. *Being a Great Mom, Raising Great Kids* was my first published book. Motherhood is one of the most important roles we will ever fill. We have the responsibility of shaping and molding the children who will one day define who we are as a community and a nation. However, as a wife, my first priority must always be to love, honor, and cherish my husband—putting my relationship with Steve second only to my relationship with God. That is the best gift I can give my child!

The seven principles of the Proverbs 31 woman are the foundational pillars of Proverbs 31 Ministries, and I believe they are key to becoming all that God intends for us to become. And the order of God first, husband second, and children third is key to a well ordered life...not just for a period of time, but for "as long as we both shall live." (For more on the seven principles, see *A Woman's Secret to a Balanced Life*, coauthored by Lysa TerKeurst and Sharon Jaynes.)

My prayer for you, dear friend, is that when all your children have grown and gone their separate ways, even though your "nest" may be empty, your home will still be full of love for your husband with deposits of treasured memories in every nook and cranny of your life. Don't wait until the kids are gone to try and catch up for the missed years. Make each day count. Right now, your marriage is becoming what it is going to be.

Yes, Valentine's Day was different that first year as empty nesters. No pink lemonade, potatoes, or heart-shaped biscuits. Instead we enjoyed a main course of special memories, a side of future hopes and dreams, and a rich dessert of intimate moments topped with the promise of more to come.

Now, back to that childhood chant. Let's learn a second verse!

First comes love,
Then comes marriage,
Then comes Susie
With the baby carriage.

Children grow up,
Kids are all gone,
Mom and Dad are still in love,
Even though they're all alone.

TWENTY

Guard Your Heart

Sitting in a waiting room, I rummaged through stacks of magazines to pass the time. *A magazine for families,* I thought as I picked up a popular title. *That ought to be safe.*

Thumbing through the pages, I went directly to the "Family Matters" column to see what the culture was teaching these days. The title? "Why You Can Love Your Husband and Brad Pitt Too." I turned back to the cover to make sure I had not inadvertently picked up *Cosmopolitan* or *The National Inquirer.* Nope. It was a magazine for families—targeted at wives and mothers.

This is some of what the author had to say.

> Last spring I found myself applying a pretty shade of pink lipstick before heading off to the nursery to buy annuals. Why the fuss? I hoped to run into the handsome gentleman who worked there… According to experts, married crushes are natural and common. As long as you don't let them develop into full-blown fantasies or consider acting upon them, these minor attractions can actually help you appreciate your spouse more…Infatuations offer a safe break from the marital routine.

> Everyday life is a bit humdrum, making it hard to maintain a passionate connection all the time...[1]

Well, friends, there is another expert on marriage who was not quoted in this article, and His teaching is the antithesis of this one. His name is Jesus. This is what He has to say about infatuation with the delivery boy, flirting with the man at the nursery, or coyly toying with a coworker in the next cubicle:

> You have heard that it was said, "Do not commit adultery." But I tell you that anyone who looks at a woman lustfully has already committed adultery with her in his heart (Matthew 5:27-28).

Looking at another man with a flirtatious eye is such a serious offense that Jesus went on to say, "If your right eye causes you to sin, gouge it out and throw it away" (Matthew 5:29). Now, don't worry, I'm not going to tell you to pluck out your eye if you do have a crush on the buff young man who bags your produce at the grocery store, but I am telling you that you might need to shop elsewhere. I am saying that if you find yourself adding a bit of lip gloss before heading to the post office where the cute blond with the steel blue eyes always greets you as though you've made his day, you need to forget the gloss and go to another post office. And that man in the next cubicle who always showers you with compliments and makes your heart skip a beat? I think Jesus is saying to change cubicles or, even more drastic, change jobs.

Perhaps you think I've gone just a bit too far. I imagine the folks listening to Jesus' advice about running from temptation thought so too. The truth is, I've never know one woman who had an affair that did not begin with a toying glance or flirtatious "innocent" bantering. Every sin begins with a thought, and every spiritual battle is won or lost at the threshold of the mind.

Let's face it. Women long to feel beautiful. After being married for a few years and having a baby or two, we begin to wonder if we are still pretty or sexually appealing. Then a man comes along who pays us a compliment and our heart skips a beat. That is natural. However, if that compliment or attention leads to infatuation, returning for more, or a "crush" as the article implied, Jesus tells us to turn and run in the opposite direction...press the delete button...and avoid a reply. "Flee from sexual immorality" (1 Corinthians 6:18). This is serious...pluck it out.

It is interesting that when Satan tempted Eve in the garden, the first step to her downfall was her eyes. "The woman *saw* that the fruit of the tree was good for food and pleasing to the *eye...*" (Genesis 3:6, emphasis added). It all began with her eyes...what she looked at. I wonder what would have happened if she had chosen to look away.

The above article had very little to do with Brad Pitt or Mel Gibson, but more to say about men we come in contact with every day. Honestly, had it been Brad or Mel, I might have had a chuckle. But this article was encouraging women to play with fire. The author went on to say:

> Whether you have a soft spot for Mel Gibson or Mel the mailman, make sure your husband knows that a crush doesn't change the way you feel about him. We all want to know that we are number one in our spouse's life. As for me, I told my husband about the man at the nursery. "Going to see your boyfriend?" he teased as I headed out the door to buy mulch. Later I assured him that while Garden Guy knew the best cure for aphids, he could never melt my heart.[2]

I read that and tried to imagine Steve saying to me, "Honey, I want to tell you that I have a crush on the checkout girl at Home Depot, but I still love you the best." I get a queasy feeling just thinking about such a conversation. And yet this is what the "family magazine" was suggesting for women of the new millennium. No wonder the divorce rate in this country is 50 percent and rising.

Charlotte's Web

What I'd like to do is put a face on the previous section. It is easy to read a story such as the one I just mentioned and think, *That would never happen to me. I would never have an affair or even be tempted to.* Sister, one of the most dangerous places we can ever be is in the place where we think, *That could never happen to me.* There is a roaring lion out there, and he is waiting for just the right moment to attack. His most common prey are those who are not on the alert. Paul says, "We are not ignorant of his [the devil's] schemes" (2 Corinthians 2:11). *But Sharon, I am a Christian,* you might be thinking. *I can skip this part.* Paul wrote to the Christians in Corinth, "I am afraid that just as Eve was deceived by the serpent's cunning, your minds may somehow be led astray from your *sincere* and *pure devotion* to Christ" (2 Corinthians 11:3, emphasis added). Read that again… *sincere* and *pure devotion.* Paul was not writing to weak or immature Christians. He was warning *mature* Christians about the seductive power of the enemy.

Let's take a look at Charlotte. This is a true story, but I have changed the names to protect Charlotte and her family. She grew up in a Christian home, attended a college Bible study, married a godly man, and was a virgin until her honeymoon night.

Growing up in a home with two older brothers and two younger brothers, Charlotte never felt good enough, pretty enough, or smart enough to measure up to her perception of what was acceptable. In an effort to receive love, Charlotte was a polite and quiet little girl who made straight A's in school and always obeyed the rules. She didn't date in high school and only had a few beaus in college. While getting her nursing degree, Charlotte met a geology major, Bill, who became one of her best friends.

Four years after graduation, Bill asked Charlotte out on their first official date, and their relationship took on a new dimension. His 6′ 5″ frame "fit well" with her 6′ stature and his large handsome hands made hers feel small and vulnerable. Bill had many qualities she had hoped to find in the man of her dreams. He was loyal to his family, devoted to Christ, and seemed to love her unconditionally. Like Charlotte, Bill had saved himself for marriage and intended to enter the marriage bed as a virgin. The only thing that was missing from the relationship was…passion. Charlotte wasn't sure that she really loved him in the way a wife should love her husband.

Charlotte was 28 when she and Bill talked of marriage. All of her friends were getting married, and some were already having children. She felt pressured that this was her best chance at love and happiness, so regardless of her many reservations, she accepted his proposal. They had a beautiful wedding that was God-centered and family-celebrated. However, as soon as she said the words "I do," Charlotte began to wish she hadn't. She was haunted by doubts from the very beginning.

"After we had been married for a few months, I remember standing in front of the mirror putting on my makeup," Charlotte explained. "The doubts were running through my mind. *Have I made a mistake? Have I married the wrong man?* Then the Holy Sprit whispered to my heart, *What if you did make a mistake? What are you going to do now?* I made a decision that I was going to love this man for the rest of my life. I had read that love was a choice, and I chose to love. Amazingly, things got better."

Three years after they were married, Charlotte and Bill had their first child. She thought, *Now I will feel fulfilled.* But that was not to be. Even though Charlotte was a pediatric nurse and told others how to take care of their children, she felt like a failure in taking care of her own. All of her insecurities came out in her efforts to parent this child. A difference in child-rearing decisions caused increased tension between Charlotte and her husband, and they disagreed at every turn.

"I felt like I was drowning and wanted Bill to rescue me somehow," she explained. "But during this time, Bill lost his job and wanted me to rescue him. We were a mess and nobody knew it. We went to church, smiled at the appropriate times, and wore the name 'Christian' like a badge."

Charlotte's heart was wide open for the enemy to attack, and there was nothing in place to guard it. She stopped studying the Bible and spending time in prayer, and she withdrew from her Christian friends. There was no accountability, just susceptibility and vulnerability.

During this trying time, Bill's cousin, Dan, began to spend a lot of time at their home. Dan was a truck mechanic, and Charlotte's two-year-old son loved to go see Uncle Dan's trucks. While Charlotte and her son visited Dan, they often talked about their marital problems.

"He listened to me. He really listened," Charlotte remembered. "One weekend Bill and I joined several family members at their cabin in the mountains. I remember Dan asking his wife if she wanted to go for a walk. She said no. Then he asked my husband if he wanted to go. He also said no. 'I'll go,' I said in a flash.

"Honestly, when Dan and I began on that walk up the mountain, I had no idea there was a slippery slope ahead. We talked about our marriage problems, his stepson, and various other issues. Bill and I never talked like that. At one point Dan held out his hand to help me down a steep incline. When I placed my hand in his, an electric shock ran through my body. We locked eyes and it was obvious the attraction was mutual."

For the next nine months, Dan and Charlotte had an emotional affair. She took her son to see Uncle Dan and his tractors often. To Bill, Charlotte seemed the happiest she had ever been in their married life, and he falsely thought it was because of him. She became pregnant with their second child, and they even went on a marriage retreat weekend with a Christian organization. He had no idea what was really going on in her heart and mind.

After the retreat the emotional affair grew into a sexual affair that lasted for seven and a half years. During that time, sexual intimacy with her husband came to a halt. Yes, he tried to approach her for about two years, but after rejection upon rejection, he gave up. Secrecy, seduction, and lies became her new way of life…which was leading to death.

"I could not believe who I had become. I was a church girl! I met my husband at InterVarsity Christian Fellowship in college. I was a virgin when I got married. I never thought this could happen to me. I tried to end the affair at least 20 times, but he had such a hold on me, I kept going back. When I was a little girl, I felt I was worthless. Now I knew I was."

After seven years of the on-again, off-again affair, Charlotte and Bill decided to change churches. At this new church Charlotte heard the truth of God rather than the "feel good" sermons she had grown accustomed to hearing. She made a decision to begin reading her Bible again, reconnecting with Christian friends, and seeking the Lord in prayer. "God, I want to end this affair once and for all," she prayed. "Please send me someone to help me and hold me accountable."

Talk to Eddy, God seemed to say.

Charlotte confided with this older woman at her new church. For the first time she told someone the entire sordid story. Lovingly, Eddy asked, "Are you ready to end it?"

"Yes," Charlotte cried. "Please help me."

Eddy prayed with Charlotte, gave her books to read, and walked her through the process of repentance and change. For the first time in her life, Charlotte understood who she was in Christ and grasped her true identity as a child of God. She had grown up in the church, but her new understanding of who she was, what she had, and where she was in Christ was the key that set her free. Eddy stood beside Charlotte as she made her final phone call to Dan and held her hand every step of the way.

Today, Charlotte is a woman set free from the bondage of sexual seduction and untangled from the web of sin. She eventually told her husband about the affair, and while it has been excruciatingly painful, the two of them are going to counseling in an effort to put their marriage back together and make it better than it ever was before.

"Charlotte," I asked "what would you tell a woman to do to avoid the same seductive trap that you fell into?" Here was her reply:

1. If you have toyed with the idea of having an affair, emotionally or physically, call a Christian friend and tell her.
2. If you feel attracted to another man, avoid contact with him.
3. Do not have a male best friend.
4. Do not tell your marriage problems to a male friend.
5. Do not confide in a male friend.
6. Do not believe the lie that life could be better with another man.
7. Do not go off alone with another man.
8. Stay connected to God through Bible study and prayer.
9. Secrets are Satan's best tool. Don't keep secrets. Once you bring something out in the open, by confessing it to another person, he loses power over you.
10. Guard your heart.

Old Faithful

King Solomon wrote, "Above all else, guard your heart, for it is the wellspring of life" (Proverbs 4:23). In a literal sense, the heart is the life-giving, blood-pumping organ located in our chests behind the upper ribs. In a metaphorical sense, the heart represents the life-giving mechanism that controls our mind, will, and emotions. It is the hidden spring of life that directs the course of our daily choices. In the Bible, the heart is the seat of joy (John 16:22), desires (Matthew 5:28), affections (Luke 24:32), perceptions (John 12:40), thoughts (Matthew 9:4), understanding (Matthew 13:15), reasoning (Mark 2:6), imagination (Luke 1:51), conscience (Acts 2:37), intentions (Hebrews 4:12), purpose (Acts 11:23), will (Romans 6:17), and faith (Mark 11:23).[3]

One summer my family traveled to Yellowstone National Park, Wyoming, and waited for over an hour to see Old Faithful shoot some 8400 gallons of boiling water 150 feet into the air. The geyser show lasted about three minutes and held a repeat performance every 76 minutes or so. The seemingly endless supply of water below the surface of the earth combined with heat and pressure have provided a watery display that has fascinated tourists for many years.

Just a few miles away, we made a quick stop to observe sulfur-filled ponds that bubbled up from the earth. These putrid smelling puddles may have been another world wonder, but we didn't see many tourists hanging around to gaze at their beauty. It was a click of the camera and then an escape from the area as quickly as possible. The stench was unbearable.

These two wellsprings reminded me of the condition of the human heart. It can be a magnificent display of faithful beauty and splendor, or a repugnant puddle of putrid disgust. With all the societal pollutants in our world today, it is easy for a heart to become contaminated. To keep a heart pure requires an endless supply of faithfulness and the steam of determination.

TWENTY-ONE

Homeland Security

After the horrific events of September 11, 2001, President George W. Bush appointed the new cabinet position of Homeland Security. It is defined as the deterrence, prevention, and preemption of, and defense against, aggression targeted at United States territory, sovereignty, population, and infrastructure, as well as the management of the consequences of such aggression and other domestic emergencies.

In a speech on July 16, 2002, in the Rose Garden, he explained how Homeland Security would deal with the threats of the twenty-first century in our country. "Our unity is a great weapon in the fight. And by acting together to create a new and single Department of Homeland Security we'll be sending the world a signal that the Congress and the administration will work together to protect the American people and to win the war on terror."[1]

As I read President Bush's description of homeland security and the perilous dangers that threaten our country, I was reminded of the danger that threatens our homes as well. There is a war going on to destroy the God-ordained institution of marriage in this country and around the world. Interestingly, my dictionary defines marriage as *the institution under which a man and a woman become legally united on a permanent basis.* Almost every word of that definition is under attack today. We need our own "homeland security" to establish the deterrence, prevention, and preemptions of, and defense against, aggression targeted against our marriages!

Men and women are typically attacked in different ways. Men are enticed by immersing their energies in their careers, escaping through sports, and being seduced by sexual temptations, whether fantasized or realized. Work and women are two of Satan's primary weapons for attacking a man's heart.

For a man to guard his heart, it usually means he must guard his eyes. For a woman to guard her heart, it means she must guard her emotions. "My coworker really listens to me," Barbara mused. "My friend Peter truly cares about my problems," Clare reflected. "Bob at the post office likes me in this red sweater," Mary pondered. Each of these thoughts sets off the "homeland security alarm."

Dear one, if we do not guard our hearts and work to keep our husbands at the top of our list, then our dreams can turn to nightmares quicker than the time it takes to press the "send" button on an e-mail.

Mighty Warrior on Patrol

The Proverbs 31 woman has represented an ideal for women throughout the ages. While she intimidates some, all would agree she is a role model worth emulating. Scripture describes her as smart, skillful, thrifty, and strong. She's a good cook, a savvy money manager, a contributor to the community, an entrepreneur, a seamstress, a blessed mother, a faithful friend, a loyal wife, and a devotee of God. As Proverbs 31:10 states, "An excellent wife, who can find? For her worth is far above jewels" (NASB). The New International Version calls her "a wife of noble character." But I personally like the Amplified Version that describes her as "a capable, intelligent, and virtuous woman." The Hebrew word that's translated "excellent" or "virtuous" can also mean "wealthy, prosperous, valiant, boldly courageous, powerful, mighty warrior."

It's the "mighty warrior" that I want to focus on for just a moment. I believe the woman of his dreams is one who is willing to fight for her marriage. She fights Satan on her knees in prayer, she fights her hectic schedule to keep her priorities in proper perspective, and she fights to guard her heart against the ungodly influences of the society in which she lives.

In verse 27, we see that the Proverbs 31 woman "watches over the ways of her household" (NKJV), or as another translation states, "she carefully watches all that goes on in her household" (NLT). The phrase "watch over" means to "hedge about as with thorns," much as a mother bird might protect her young with the thorny rim of a nest. These same words are also used in the Bible as a military term, such as to watch over a city.[2]

I envision the wife of noble character walking around the wall fortifying her home, fully equipped to take on any enemy that threatens to invade her marriage. But we can't assume the enemy is always some outside force. I believe the greatest enemy can be what happens in our own hearts and minds.

King David's Demise

King David was called a man after God's own heart (1 Samuel 3:14). However, there was a point in his life when he let his guard down around that God-fearing heart of his, and he ended up having an affair and conspiring murder.

David had gone from a mere shepherd boy to becoming king. One day when all his men were off at war, he decided to stay back at the castle and lollygag around. While strolling on the roof to get a breath of fresh air, he noticed his neighbor's wife, Bathsheba, taking a bath on the roof of her home. David had grown accustomed to getting what he wanted, and he wanted

Bathsheba. A few months later, she reported that she was pregnant with his child. In a panic to cover his sin, David ordered Bathsheba's husband, Uriah, to the front line of battle and then ordered the other men to withdraw. As planned, Uriah was killed and David took Bathsheba to be his wife. From that time on, David's life took a downward spiral.

What Can We Learn from David's Lack of Guarding His Heart?

Many events in the Bible are recorded as examples for future generations (1 Corinthians 10:11). Let's take a look at how we can guard our hearts by examining how King David did not guard his.

He was in the wrong place at the wrong time. The story begins "In the spring, at the time when kings go off to war" (2 Samuel 11:1). David was supposed to be off at war, but instead he stayed behind and shirked his duties. In order to guard our hearts, we must make sure we are not putting ourselves in a situation to be tempted. Have you ever found yourself at the wrong place at the wrong time—not by accident, but by choice?

He was lonely and vulnerable. I've often heard the phrase "It's lonely at the top." But I can assure you it can be lonely at the bottom and all in-between. If you are lonely, seek out the company of a female friend. Just as God sent Mary to Elizabeth and Ruth to Naomi, He continues to use women to encourage women. Seeking companionship with a man is treading on dangerous ground.

He knew what was right and ignored his better judgment. After David had sinned with Bathsheba, the prophet Nathan came to him and told him about a wealthy man who had many sheep, but he had stolen a poor man's one and only sheep. David said, "As surely as the LORD lives, the man who did this deserves to die!" (2 Samuel 12:5). The prophet responded, "You are the man!" (verse 7). David knew what he was doing was wrong, but he proceeded anyway.

God will always provide a way of escape. There were many steps to the process of David's sin. At any point he could have stopped, but he didn't. God will always provide a way of escape for any temptation (1 Corinthians 10:13). The sooner we heed His warning, the easier it will be to turn and go in the opposite direction. As soon as a tempting thought enters our mind, we need to press the mental "delete" key to guard our heart.

No one is above temptation. David was a very godly man. He wrote psalms and truly loved the Lord. And yet he still committed adultery and murder. I wonder, when he was praising God during his coronation, if he ever imagined in his wildest dreams that he would fall in such a way. Paul reminds us in 1 Corinthians 10:12-13: "So, if you think you are standing firm, be careful that you don't fall! No temptation has seized you except what is common to man. And God is faithful; he will not let you be tempted beyond what you can bear. But when you are tempted, he will also provide a way out so that you can stand up under it."

The Holy Spirit will convict us. David's downfall took place over at least a year's period of time. How many times do you think the Holy Spirit warned him of his sin? Nothing should frighten us more than to know that we have the choice to shut out God's warning and the Holy Spirit's convicting.

Honestly, I wish the story of David's sin was not in the Bible. I'd much rather remember him as the giant slayer who loved God more than life itself. But God wants us to know that no one is immune to temptation. David's fall is a picture of what can happen to anyone who does not guard his or her heart.

Now, Go Love Your Husband

I had been speaking at a women's conference in Virginia and concluding my final session. The audience applauded. I smiled, waved a goodbye, and made my way to my seat filled with joy over what God had done. It was a perfect ending to the end of a storybook spiritual retreat. But then God prodded me. *You're not done,* He seemed to say. *There's one more thing you need to tell the ladies before they disperse and make their way home.*

What, Lord? What is it? I asked.

Get back up there and tell them to go home and love their husbands, He said.

But that doesn't have anything to do with what I've been talking about all weekend, I argued.

Get back up there and tell them to go home and love their husbands, He said again.

I walked back up on stage and tapped the shoulder of the event coordinator, who was making closing comments.

"I'm sorry," I said, "but God wants me to tell the ladies one more thing."

She handed me the microphone, and I said, "Ladies, God wants me to tell you to go home and love your husband. You have been here at this wonderful retreat center for three days—singing praises, studying God's Word, bonding with sisters in Christ, and falling more and more in love with Jesus Christ. Now, He wants you to go home and show how much you love Him by loving your husband.

"Some husbands will feel a bit alienated because of your spiritual high. Some of you are going home knowing Jesus as your Savior for the very first time and your husband may question where he fits in your newfound faith. Do you realize that your spiritual excitement could make your husband jealous or cause him to question his place in your heart? God wants you to remove that uncertainty by returning home and loving your husband as you've never loved him before. That's what God wants you to do for Him.

"Know this. When you love your husband, you are loving God."

There was not a dry eye in the room among the married women. Many loved the Lord, but many were not loving their husbands. If they obeyed God's commission, I bet their husbands were anxious to sign their wives up for next year's retreat!

Yes, it is imperative that we love God first and foremost in our lives. Proverbs 31:30 says, "Charm is deceptive and beauty is fleeting; but a woman who fears the LORD is to be praised." But loving our husband should run such a close second that it is hard to tell where one stops and the other begins.

"What a man desires is unfailing love," King Solomon explained (Proverbs 19:22). He wants to know that he has a special, permanent place in your heart reserved only for him. Jesus is not his competition, but the One who encourages you to love your man with all you've got and then some.

Twenty-Five Ways to Safeguard Your Marriage

When it comes to in-laws...
1. Have a plan of when in-laws will visit and how long they will stay.
2. Take a walk if you find yourself growing frustrated.
3. Destroy the list of negative character flaws or irritations.
4. Create a list of positive attributes and admirable qualities.
5. Let negative comments roll off your back.
6. Prepare for the holidays by communicating expectations ahead of time.
7. Pray.

When it comes to children...
8. Get away once or twice a year without the children.
9. Get creative and plan a date night once a week.
10. Get lovey-dovey and stop what you're doing to give him a hug when he comes in the door in the evening.
11. Get intentional about looking for ways to show him he's still number one in your life.
12. Get personal by having intimate conversations with no interruptions.

13. Get your husband involved in caring for the children.
14. Get practical and think of ways to reignite the flame of passion once the baby comes. (Perhaps take a nap when baby naps.)

When it comes to other men...
15. Have an accountability partner (a Christian friend) with whom you can admit any tempting thoughts. If need be, ask her to pray for you.
16. Avoid contact with any man to whom you feel attracted, either emotionally or physically.
17. Avoid having a male best friend.
18. Avoid telling your marriage problems to another man.
19. Avoid having a male confidant.
20. Do not believe Satan's lies that life could be better with another man or that you've simply married the wrong person.
21. Avoid being alone with another man (whether socially or professionally).
22. Avoid seemingly innocent Internet relationships.
23. Stay connected to God through Bible study and prayer.
24. Stay emotionally connected to your husband.
25. Pray for your husband daily.

Section Six

Encourages Him

⤶

TWENTY-TWO

The Power of a Word

William met Claire while he was earning his master's degree in graphic art and design. In the early dating days, their conversations were filled with praise and admiration for each other. When William gave Claire a framed original poem in calligraphy with a beautifully designed border, she showered him with praise for his talent, thoughtfulness, and time.

"Oh, William," she gushed, "you shouldn't have spent so much time and effort to make this for me. It is the most beautiful poem I have ever read—and the calligraphy, how do you do that?"

"It's no big deal, really," he said. "Anyone could learn how to do it if they tried."

"I don't believe that for a minute. You are so talented and I'm proud of you."

After several months William and Claire were married. At first all was well, but after a year or two, Claire began to feel William wasn't progressing quickly enough in his job at the television studio doing graphic design for commercials and the evening news programs. The compliments grew fewer and fewer and the sarcastic jabs grew more frequent.

"I think you need to have a talk with your boss," she nagged. "You've been working at this job for three years and he hasn't given you a raise yet. Maybe you should look into working somewhere else that pays better. Kathy's husband, Paul, is a graphic designer, and he makes twice what you make."

After a while Claire refrained from giving any encouraging words to William, and he refrained from talking about his work at all.

Meanwhile, William began to spend more time at the office with his coworker Jane.

"You are so talented, William," Jane said. "I was so impressed with your layout on that story on the stock market yesterday. Only you could take a bunch of numbers and make them look exciting and attractive! You're the best graphic designer we have."

"Boy, I wish my wife thought so. She just doesn't understand how much pressure I'm under every day. Claire thinks I'm not trying hard enough to move up the corporate ladder."

"Not trying hard enough!" Jane exclaimed. "Doesn't she know how hard this business is? She should be proud to have a hardworking husband like you. There are plenty of women who would be overjoyed to have someone as kind and considerate."

Jane touched William's hand and finished her thought. "Me, for one."

It wasn't long after that William and Jane began their affair.

While this is a fictitious story, it is played out in homes and offices all around the world on a daily basis. The names and occupations may be different, but the longings are the same. The reality is, if we aren't willing to offer encouraging words to our husbands, there are plenty of women who would love to do it for us.

As we have already seen in section three, the woman of your man's dreams is one who adores, admires, and appreciates him. Kissing cousins to admiration is giving the gift of encouragement. My dictionary defines encouragement as *to give courage or confidence to, to raise the hopes of, to help on by sympathetic advice and interest, to promote or stimulate.* The primary way we encourage others is by the words we speak. William Barclay once said:

> One of the highest duties is the duty of encouragement. It is easy to laugh at men's ideas; it is easy to pour cold water on their enthusiasm; it is easy to discourage others. The world is full of discouragers. We have a Christian duty to encourage one another. Many a time a word of praise or thanks or appreciation or cheer has kept a man on his feet. Blessed is the man (or woman) who speaks such a word.[1]

I believe there is nothing more powerful than words. God spoke the world into existence. He said, "Let there be..." and there was. Of all the living creatures that God created, human beings are the only ones that have the gift of words, and we can choose to use those words for good or for evil.

In the New Testament, James compared the tongue to three very small objects that control three very large forces: a bit in a horse's mouth that controls whether the animal stops, starts, or turns to the left or right, a rudder on a ship that directs its course, and a spark that ignites a forest fire. Likewise, our words can cause someone to start or stop, direct the entire course of a life, or set a heart aflame.

> *I wish my wife understood how fragile a man's ego is.* —Stan

> *Men are encouraged when they are reminded about their accomplishments.* —Douglas

> *My wife is 100 percent on my side and is actively working to help, support, and encourage me in achieving my goals. She makes my home a safe haven*

where peace, rest, and joy give me a break from the burdens I deal with outside the home. I really love her for doing that! —Winston

I wish my wife better understood my feelings of success and failure, hopes and aspirations, fears and concerns, motivations and deterrents, prayers and wishes, pleasures and disappointments. I long for her not to long for something other than what is. —John

Salve to the Hurting Soul

There is much in print today about low self-esteem in women. However, I see that same problem in men. They are less likely to expose or admit their need for encouragement, I believe, because it goes against the world's idea of masculinity. Men are taught to be tough, have thick skin, and not need kind words. But they crave admiration and are attracted to it like bees to honey. King Solomon wrote, "Pleasant words are a honeycomb, sweet to the soul and healing to the bones" (Proverbs 16:24), but "reckless words pierce like a sword" (Proverbs 12:18).

Our men may never tell us about the wounds that were inflicted on them as children by ill-spoken words. "You are such a slob." "You'll never amount to anything." "Why can't you make good grades the way I did when I was in school?" "Look how scrawny you are!" "Don't let those guys pick on you like you're some kind of coward. Fight back!" "You're a loser and you will always be a loser." "When I was your age, I was already working a part-time job, going to school, and playing on the football team."

Ken shared such a painful childhood memory with me. He remembers trying out for the junior high football team. He didn't like the sport—or any sport, for that matter—but he did so to please his dad. During tryouts, Ken's dad stood on the sidelines and watched as a young man threw a pass to his son. Ken didn't get his arms up in time and the ball bonked him in the head. His dad simply looked at him in disgust and turned to walk away. Later that evening his father said, "You're good for nothing." Twenty-five years later, Ken still feels as though he's "good for nothing."

Encouragement involves affirming an individual. To affirm means to "make firm, to declare positively, to assert, to confirm, to ratify, to validate." We can do all that...with our words.

Let's go back to the beginning of time once again. Adam was very impressed with this new creation called woman, so much so that he forgot his role as leader and gave in to his wife's enticement to disobey God. Why did Satan tempt Eve rather than Adam? Was it because she could be deceived easier, or was it because he knew if he could cause Eve to disobey, she could persuade her husband to follow suit? I believe Satan knew the incredible influence Eve had on her man. If he could get to the woman, then the woman could get to the man. Adam's desire for Eve overrode his desire to obey God. Oh, ladies, do you understand the responsibility we have to guard our words? God has given us great power, and we can use that influence for good or evil.

I saw a placard recently that read "I always have the last word with my wife. It's 'Yes, dear.'" We chuckle—but it's not really funny, is it? Perhaps those are the very words Adam said to Eve.

> *The woman of my dreams understands that I am not as "strong" emotionally as she thinks. I need her as much as she needs me, maybe even more. —John*

> *I wish my wife understood the pressure that is on me at work and at home every day—to perform, to do, to plan, to protect, to be the "bad guy" with the kids, to discipline. I long for time with just her and me—no kids around. —Ron*

> *I wish my wife understood how vulnerable I really am. —Donald*

Building Blocks or Stumbling Blocks?

King Solomon wrote that "the tongue has the power of life and death" (Proverbs 18:21). He also said that "the wise woman builds her house, but with her own hands the foolish one tears hers down" (Proverbs 14:1). I don't think we need to use our hands to tear down our houses. We can do that quite well with our tongues.

The question we wives need to ask ourselves is, do our words bring life or death? Do they build up or tear down? Take a look at these two lists of words and see which more appropriately fits your words on any given day.

Words That Build Up	Words That Tear Down
I've been thinking about you all day.	Just forget it.
What can I do for you today?	You never help me around the house.
How can I pray for you today?	You're always in a bad mood.
The best part of my day is when you come home.	All you ever do is complain.
You are one of God's most precious gifts to me.	Who do you think you are?
Thank you.	We never have enough money.
I'm sorry.	I can never please you.
You are so wonderful.	How many times do I have to tell you?

You look so handsome in that shirt.	All you ever think about is yourself.
You make my day bright.	That was stupid.
I don't feel complete without you.	You don't own me.
You are my best friend.	You're impossible.
I thought about you all day.	I can't believe you said that.
Thank you for loving me.	What do you want now?
Thank you for taking such good care of me.	I guess I expect too much.
You're my knight in shining armor.	You can't do anything right.
I will always love you.	You know where the door is.
You are so tough.	You are such a big baby.
I trust your decision.	You never listen to me.
I can always count on you.	You're so irresponsible.
You make me feel special.	Now you know how I feel.
What would you like to do?	It's all about you, isn't it?
I prize every moment we're together.	I can't do this anymore.
I see God's fingerprints all over your life.	What's wrong with you anyhow?
You are such an inspiration to so many people.	Do you always have to be right?

TWENTY-THREE

Don't Try to Out-Man Your Man

There are certain laws of nature that are undeniable. If you drop a rock from a tall building, it will fall to the ground. We call that gravity. If you spin around in circles for an exorbitant amount of time, you're going to become dizzy. We call this upsetting our equilibrium. If a woman tries to out-man her man, he will feel emasculated. I call that reality. It is a law of nature that a man wants to feel manly. With the rise of homosexuality in the past few decades, some will be quick to disagree. However, I feel many men turn to homosexuality because they feel they have been out-manned by women, given up, and chosen the path of least resistance.

Since the 1960s, the women's liberation movement has made an attempt to make women become more like men by implying that being a woman isn't good enough. "We can do everything they can do—and even better," women have taunted, chanted, and cheered. Yes, we've come a long way, baby, and it's not looking too good. Since 1953, the divorce rate has climbed from 20 percent to the present 50 percent.[1]

My friend Barbara watched an exchange between her eight-year-old daughter and ten-year-old son. "Michael, can you open this for me?" Christine asked.

Michael puffed up his chest like a toad. "Sure," he said with great pride. "Hey, Dad, let me borrow your pocketknife." Barbara even noticed he asked with a certain gruffness and lower-than-normal tone in his voice.

Even at ten years old, little boys are asking, "Am I man enough to make it? Do you think I'm tough?"

I can promise you this. That big boy who lives in your house, the one who sleeps beside you every night, he's asking the same questions: *Do you think I'm man enough? Do you think I have what it takes?* What has been your response? Are you encouraging him in his masculinity?

Men want to prove their masculinity, and if they can't prove it at home, they will search for other means to do so. It may be an affair with someone at the office, the secret seduction of Internet chat rooms or pornography, drinking with the guys, an obsession with competitive sports, swearing, sarcasm, criticism, and so on. He's asking, "Do you think I'm manly?"

When I say a woman shouldn't try and out-man a man, I do not mean she is to be a passive mamby-pamby weakling. Al Janssen, author of *Marriage Masterpiece,* notes, "Men long for a strong woman who will make them look good, not weak. What if Eve had asked the serpent, 'Why are you questioning God?' What if she had turned to Adam and said, 'Something's not right here. We shouldn't listen to this beast.' Rarely are men attracted to a strong-willed woman who always demands her own way, but they admire the woman of noble character who maintains her femininity, honors her husband, yet can see to the heart of the situation and give her man the information he needs to act appropriately."[2]

Take a look at the wife of noble character in Proverbs 31:10-31. While she respected her husband and gave him great confidence to succeed, she had quite a list of accomplishments herself. This gal ran a family business, purchased real estate, ran a winery, invested profits, supervised servants, and raised children who called her blessed. She was industrious, thrifty, competent, strong, energetic, confident, trustworthy, intelligent, resourceful, gracious, courageous, noble, intelligent, loving, and compassionate. She didn't sit around saying "yes, sir" and "no, sir." Yet she respected her husband and he had a seat of respect and honor at the city gate where the leaders congregated.

It is the man who is honored and encouraged at home who has the confidence to excel away from home. If his wife continually beats him at cards, beats him at basketball, beats him in his earning potential, beats him in making repairs at home, and beats him in solving problems, he will seek elsewhere to "win." Don't be surprised if such a man takes up camping in the Ozarks or climbing Mt. Everest. Is the hair on the back of your neck bristling with that last sentence? Does that go against everything your liberated sisters have taught you? I suspect it does. That's okay.

> *I desire for my wife to support and honor me, not overshadow or overrun me.* —Curt

> *The woman of my dreams is happy and secure in the idea that she is created to complement me with her femininity and uniqueness as a woman, and she does not try to compete with masculine roles and characteristics.* —Bill

> *I wish my wife understood how much I need to feel respected. I know it is the antithesis of what the culture promotes and portrays. Men are typically treated as irresponsible, angry children.* —Paul

And as a side note here, your sons and daughters are watching. Yes, we may have produced strong daughters, but at what cost? "The wreaths you receive from your outstanding performance could create the chains that your sons or your daughters will find controlling their lives."[3] They are listening to the words you speak and how you speak them. You are providing a living example of how they will inevitably treat their own spouses.

But what if you *are* smarter? What if you *are* better at sports? What if you *do* earn more money than he does? I suggest you discover what *he* is good at and accentuate the positive. "Honey, it always amazes me how you know how to fix cars like that." "Honey, how do you ever remember all those numbers at work?" "Honey, I have never known a man who could trim bushes and keep a yard so immaculate. I am so lucky to have a man around like you!" "You could give lessons on how to be a good husband." "I am so lucky to be married to such an incredible lover."

Competition has never been a problem in my house, especially when it comes to sports. In the fifth grade, when I was forced to play on the Pink Panthers softball team, I opted for right field because no one could hit the ball that far and I felt I was safe from humiliation. I decided early on that if a game had a ball in it, that game was not for me.

However, when I was in college, I tried snow skiing. Amazingly, I took to the slopes like a duck to water and swished and swooshed down the mountains with agility and speed. My friends were amazed. "Who is that ski-masked girl?" they asked. It's been over 20 years, and I still enjoy tooling down the mountain with the crisp wind blowing through my hair. The only explanation for this "athletic" ability is that there is no ball and no competition. It's just me and the mountain. As I said earlier, my husband and son have also taken up snow skiing. However, for them it's competing with each other all the way to the bottom of the hill.

Men are wired to compete. They play to win. Girls today are encouraged to compete in every sport available. I'm not saying that is good or bad; I just know it is difficult to trust someone with your heart if you see her as a competitor.

One of the greatest struggles in our marriage has been that we should be mutually more tolerant and less demanding about little things which often are not that important. We should work harder to avoid words and attitudes which may be abrasive and have a negative impact on our marital fellowship. —Jim

I just want peace—less nagging and more trying to get along. —Russ

All men need more encouragement. They need to know that they have at least one big-time fan. —Gene

Team Spirit

When my son was a sophomore, he played on the school basketball team. During one of the games, I noticed a man on our side videotaping the game and a man on the opposing side videotaping the game.

"Steve, what are those two men doing?" I asked.

"Well, the guy on our side is videoing the game so the boys can look at it later and improve their weaknesses. The man on the other side is from the team we are playing next week. He is videoing the game so our competitors will see our vulnerabilities and know where to attack."

Do we see our husband's weaknesses as vulnerabilities to attack or as areas where we can help make him strong? Are we playing on the same team, wearing the same jersey, and following the same game plan? If we want to become the wife of his dreams, we need to sign a "no compete" clause and make sure we're players for the same side.

County fairs are known for their various contests. At one particular fair, a pulling contest was used to determine who had the strongest horse. The first-place horse moved a sled weighing 4500 pounds, and the second-place horse moved a sled that weighed 4000. The owners were curious as to how much the two could pull if they worked together, so they hitched them up and added more weight to the sled. To everyone's surprise, the horses pulled 12,000 pounds.[4]

The word for combined strength, which was demonstrated in the two horses working together, is "synergism." It means doing more together than two can do alone. What a beautiful picture of a marriage's power when the husband and wife work together for common goals.

God created woman to complete man, not to compete with man. He instructed them to "be fruitful and multiply." This task cannot be accomplished alone...it takes two working together for common goals. Whether it is multiplying your family, multiplying your finances, or multiplying your happy memories, working together on the same team will produce a marriage that is fruitful...and, oh, that fruit can be so sweet!

> *I always wanted a "helpmate" as described in Genesis. A woman I could team with where she and I could accomplish more for God as a couple than either of us could separately. That means that we don't share identical strengths and weaknesses, but that her strengths complement my weaknesses and vice versa.* —Paul

> *Women need to understand that a man wants a woman who will be his "dream wife," not only on their wedding day but on each day of their relationship, becoming more and more his "dream" with him. Even men who did not really think about a "dream wife" want a wife who will become someone to help him take a stand against the rest of the world. A man does not want a wife who will take a stand against him.* —Clyde

TWENTY-FOUR

What You Plant Is What You Grow

After Steve and I built our dream home, we hauled in truck-loads of rich topsoil and spread it over our rocky ground. Then we planted thousands of tiny fescue grass seeds. After several weeks of watering, slender blades of green began to push their way through the dirt in search of the sunlight. Within six weeks, our yard was a carpet of luscious grass that beckoned us to kick off our shoes and walk barefoot across the lawn.

The following spring, I noticed a few unwelcome visitors in my prize lawn: dandelions, crabgrass, and ground ivy.

"Steve," I asked, "where did those weeds come from? We surely didn't plant them!"

"The weeds came from seeds that blew in from other places. Mostly from our neighbors' yards," he answered.

After the grass came up, all the green blended together nicely, and we hardly noticed the weeds. However, the next spring, we had more weeds and less grass. By the fourth spring, we knew that if we didn't apply some sort of weed control, soon we would have a yard full of weeds and no grass at all.

Thinking of our lawn reminds me of the words we speak in our marriages. During the dating and courting days, we tend to shower our prospective mate with seeds of encouraging words, compliments, adoration, and praise. After we are married, the weeds begin to creep in and sprout up: a sarcastic comment here, a critical jab there, and a nagging spirit in-between. As time passes, if we do not give attention to the weed problem, we are in danger of having a yard full of weeds with no grass at all—a marriage full of criticism with not an encouraging word to be heard.

Anabel Gillham, author of *The Confident Woman*, tells about a time when an elderly man came up to her after a conference. During the session she had mentioned a couple she had counseled where the man yelled in frustration that in his 13-year marriage, his wife had never praised him in front of anyone.

"You remember the man whose wife had not praised him in 13 years, Anabel?"

"Yes," she said.

He twisted his hat in his hand, looked up, and then down again. There were tears in his eyes. When he regained his composure, he continued.

"Would you believe 39 years, Anabel?"

"I beg your pardon?" she asked.

"Yes. Thirty-nine long years…"

She talked to him for quite a while. He told her that his wife had never been content with him, that he had tried to please her but just couldn't seem to meet her standards. Then, as though he were confessing to someone who could forgive him, he told her how he had visited his sister recently for a month, alone. His wife chose not to go with him. While he was there, he went to a senior citizens barbecue and sat by a woman who simply listened to him and responded to him with pleasant words and interesting questions. They saw each other several times during his visit. "We never touched each other, and I can't explain what happened to me when we were together…walking, talking, sitting at the card table drinking coffee. I was content. I was special. I didn't entertain any ideas about leaving my wife, Anabel. I would never do that. But it was awfully hard to go back home."[1]

Men need encouraging words from the women in their lives, starting with their mothers, continuing with girlfriends, and hopefully ending with their wives. It is a God-given need they never outgrow, whether they are eight days old or eighty years old.

I remember the children's poem:

Every plant has little seeds
That make others of its kind.
Apple seeds make apple trees
And they'll do it every time.

Seeds make flowers, shrubs, and trees.
Seeds make ferns, vines, and weeds.
What you plant is what you grow.
So be careful what you sow.

Author Unknown

What kind of seeds are you planting in your marriage?

A man dreams of being needed and wanted by a wife. There are times when I know my wife looks up to me, respects me, and honors me. That is when I love her the most and feel the best about myself as well. When I feel strong, I am strong. More than any other person in the world, she holds the key to my confidence. —Al

Breaking Up Fallow Ground

Each spring, when I plant petunias, begonias, and impatiens around the perimeter of my home, I have to go in and break up the hardened soil and add some fresh nutritious topsoil to the mix. If I try to plant the tiny seedlings into the hardened soil, they will have difficulty pushing their hairlike roots through the dirt in order to grow.

I realize we have already touched on the necessity of forgiveness in a healthy marriage relationship, but I feel I must mention it again. Perhaps one of the most common reasons for a wife withholding encouraging words from her husband is unforgiveness. A seed of resentment can grow into a well-established root of bitterness that produces hurtful words and destroys a marriage like kudzu in a forest. Maybe you've been hurt. Maybe you feel your husband doesn't deserve encouraging words. After all, what's he done to encourage you lately?

A young lady went to Florence Littauer with a tale of hostility toward her husband. As she poured out all his misdeeds, they seemed so trivial that Florence asked her when her feelings of hatred had started. She replied quickly, "I was mad at him before we even got married."

Her fiancé had written a letter instructing her to find a car for their honeymoon trip. She had answered that it was his responsibility to provide transportation and, besides, his family had three cars while hers had only one. He made it clear: "If you want to marry me, you had better find a car!" She found a car, but she vowed she would never forget his injustice.

She looked up at Florence with bitterness lining her face and said, "In case you don't believe me, I'll show you the letter he wrote." She reached into her handbag and pulled out a worn and tattered envelope that had moved from bag to bag for ten years. As she handed it to her, she said, "I always carry it with me so I won't forget."[2]

I doubt that any of us carry around a letter in our pocketbooks, but I wonder how many of us carry around a letter in our hearts. The writer of Hebrews warns, "See to it that no one misses the grace of God and that no bitter root grows up to cause trouble and defile many" (Hebrews 12:15). A bitter root is one that bears bitter fruit. A bitter heart is one that bears a bitter woman with bitter words.

"No good tree bears bad fruit, nor does a bad tree bear good fruit. Each tree is recognized by its own fruit. People do not pick figs from thornbushes, or grapes from briers. The good man brings good things out of the good stored up in his heart, and the evil man brings evil things out of the evil stored up in his heart. For out of the overflow of his heart his mouth speaks" (Luke 6:43). What determines the tree? The fruit—bitter or sweet.

> *The woman of my dreams is one who would encourage me to develop my talents to their fullest extent, and I also for her. —Jim*

> *My wife is very supportive of my career and very encouraging. The world would be a much nicer place if more women were as sweet as my wife. —Al*

> *I long to know my purpose in life and do something great, but my wife can't really do anything about that other than support me in my efforts to discover it. —Rob*

The Proverbial Wife

The book of Proverbs has much to say about wives and words. (This is a section you do not want your husband to see!)

- Like a gold ring in a pig's snout is a beautiful woman who shows no discretion (Proverbs 11:22).

- A quarrelsome wife is like a constant dripping (Proverbs 19:13).

- Better to live on a corner of the roof than share a house with a quarrelsome wife (Proverbs 21:9; worth repeating: Proverbs 25:24).

- Better to live in a desert than with a quarrelsome and ill-tempered wife (Proverbs 21:19).

- A quarrelsome wife is like a constant dripping on a rainy day; restraining her is like restraining the wind or grasping oil with the hand (Proverbs 27:15-16).

Enough already. We get the picture!

On a more positive note, King Lemuel's mother described the type of woman she hoped her son would one day marry: "A wife of noble character who can find? She is worth far more than rubies. Her husband has full confidence in her and lacks nothing of value. She brings him good, not harm, all the days of her life…her children arise and call her blessed; her husband also, and he praises her: 'Many women do noble things, but you surpass them all'" (Proverbs 31:10-12,28-29).

Let's go back to a passage of Scripture we've already visited, Ephesians 5:33. We've already spent some time discussing a man's need for respect, but let's look at this verse in the Amplified Version of the Bible. "Let the wife see that she respects and reverences her husband [that she notices him, regards him, honors him, prefers him, venerates, and esteems him; and that she defers to him, praises him, and loves and admires him exceedingly]" (AMP).

Let's look at these directives and see how our words stack up.

Do We		Do We
Respect	or	Show contempt
Reverence	or	Dishonor
Notice	or	Ignore
Regard	or	Disregard
Honor	or	Humiliate
Prefer	or	Exclude
Venerate	or	Belittle
Esteem	or	Mock
Defer	or	Usurp

Praise	or	Criticize
Love	or	Hate
Admire	or	Ridicule[3]

How did you do? Is there room for improvement? I like what Robert Louis Stevenson said: "Make the most of the best and the least of the worst." What a wonderful adage when it comes to the words of a woman to her man.

Remember Don and Jona in section one? I talked to Don about how Jona's hurtful words affected him as a man.

"When I met Jona at the beach retreat," Don explained, "I was struck by her vivacious, fun attitude. Oh, and did I mention she looked great in her purple bathing suit? (This is 20 years later, and he still remembers the color!) She stole my heart, and as soon as we got home from the retreat, I called and asked her out.

"I had always been a people pleaser. At first I was always trying to please my parents, then I moved to pleasing my friends, and when I met Jona, I always tried to please her as well. We were soon married and I couldn't have been happier. She was so encouraging, loving, and supportive. After a few years of marriage and several poor financial decisions, I began to see her lose her respect for me. That was most evident in the words she spoke.

"In the past everything I touched turned to gold. I was president of the student body association, won athletic awards, and succeeded in business. As a result, I overpromised to Jona and expected her to trust me. Jona was the one person I wanted approval from and the one person from whom I was not getting it. She grew frustrated, angry, and bitter toward me. She also withdrew physically, which was the crowning blow to my manhood.

"Jona said things like, 'If you cared about us, you wouldn't make all these bad decisions. You're a loser. You're worthless.'

"I'm not putting all the blame of our past marriage problems on Jona. I was shooting for the moon instead of a ten-yard gain. I was trying to hit a home run instead of a base hit. But honestly, once I realized Jona had lost respect for me, I felt the marriage was over. Her words cut too deep, and no bandage could stop the bleeding."

I asked Don what could have made a difference and prevented the eventual separation and divorce.

"If she had said, 'I'm with you, Don' or 'Let's work on this together' or 'How can I help?' it would have made all the difference in the world. I didn't feel like we were on the same team. Instead, she said, 'If you don't fix it, I will.' Instead of constantly pointing out my failures, because believe me, I knew what they were, encouraging words would have made all the difference.

"At one point," Don said with tears in his eyes, "I found a list of 80 things that Jona didn't like about me and three things she did like. That list broke my heart. She had no intention of me finding the list, but I happened across it one day when I was looking for something. That was the final nail in the coffin. Jona had nothing but disdain for me. A marriage without respect is no marriage. I saw no hope."

After Don and Jona's divorce, he met a woman who gave him all the adoration and encouragement that his wife had not. She was gentle, soft-spoken, and affectionate. She hung on his shoulder, smiled at him, and was very affirming. While he did not consider her a beauty, her beautiful spirit was a breath of fresh air.

You've already read how God miraculously brought Don and Jona back together. She made a commitment to give Don her BEST and never cut him down again. He was drawn back to the wife of his youth and now revels in the sweetness of her words and deeds.

"Don," I asked, "what advice do you have for a woman who is withholding encouraging words or perhaps cutting her husband down with critical jabs?"

"I don't think any single thing takes away a man's strength of character more than the loss of respect," he said. "Don't dwell on his weaknesses, but dwell on the positives. Men are in a fight for our lives. We are at war mentally. We're out there trying to conquer the world. A man needs to know that home is a safe place to be instead of feeling like you're leaving one battle for another."

Maybe you have not been giving encouraging words to your husband lately. Perhaps it has been so long you've forgotten how. I hope Don and Jona's story stirs your heart to build up that man of yours and become the woman of his dreams.

Think back to when you were dating. What did you admire about that young man who captured your heart? Look for an opportunity to praise him, but make sure it is genuine. Find one attribute, character trait, or task he does well, and begin there. If you are out of practice, this may be difficult at first. But I can promise you, it will become easier with time, especially when you see the results on your husband's face and his attitude toward you.

Also, if your husband has heard critical words for many years, it may take him a while to trust the new you. One day I had a mattress delivered to my home. The delivery man placed the work order on a beautiful piece of furniture in our foyer, took out a ballpoint pen, and then bore down to sign his name on the delivery line. When he removed the paper, his name was left engraved on the table's smooth surface.

I had the table resurfaced, but the refinisher told me he had to go back several times to sand it. Just when he thought he had the name removed, it would pop back up again. That's how it may be with our words. It might take some time to erase the harmful effects our hurtful words have wrought, but with enough love and encouragement, we can make our husbands shining and new.

Paul wrote, "Let no foul or polluting language, nor evil word, nor unwholesome or worthless talk [ever] come out of your mouth, but only such [speech] as is good and beneficial to the spiritual progress of others, as is fitting to the need and the occasion, that it may be a blessing and give grace (God's favor) to those who hear it" (Ephesians 4:29 AMP). As Florence Littauer says in her book *Silver Boxes,* "Our words should be like gifts to each other, little silver boxes with bows on top."[4] For some of us, a gag present would be a welcomed relief!

Friday is droop day at my house. I tend to only water my plants once a week and by the end of the week, the Peace Lily in the den resembles a haggard old woman, and African violets look as though they are on their way to their mother country. After I make my rounds with the watering can, the plants stand at attention and perk back up as if to say, "Thank you, thank you, thank you."

Is your husband a bit droopy? Are his leaves beginning to wilt or his branches beginning to sag? I suggest watering him with a good dose of encouraging words and watch him perk back up and spring to life.

I wish my wife better understood the areas I am insecure in, things like not feeling as though I measure up around a lot of other men. —Randal

Men want to be encouraged and validated. We need to hear we are the best—from the bedroom to the marketplace. You can get a man to do almost anything with a little bragging. Wise up, ladies, and blow a little sunshine on your man and watch what happens! —Brad

I don't have much confidence in myself, but my wife's being consistently positive with me and giving me praise and admiration helps. —James

TWENTY-FIVE

Chief Cheerleader or Chief Critic?

Ted met Beverly in 1975 at the University of Georgia. He was immediately attracted to her vivacious spirit and zest for life. Ted and Bev were married in 1978, each having one year of undergraduate studies to complete. They were both sending themselves to school and lived off of love and a few student loans. After graduation, Ted enrolled into chiropractic school. Three years later, he became known as Dr. Theodore Greve. On a wing and a promise, the young couple, with new baby in tow, moved to North Carolina where Ted set up his chiropractic practice.

"I loved the interaction with the patients," Ted explained to me, "but after a few years, I grew tired of the repetition of the treatment. Something inside me began to long for more. I couldn't imagine being in this profession for the rest of my life. My heart's desire was to go back to school—perhaps to study law. But what would Bev say? That was my biggest hurdle."

After four years of building his practice, Ted and Bev were well on their way to acquiring the American Dream. With a six-figure income, two kids (a boy and a girl), a two-car garage, a beautiful home, country club membership, and an abundance of friends, Bev had everything a girl could want...except one thing—a happy husband.

"Finally, I broached the subject of returning to school," Ted continued. "I told Bev I was miserable doing what I was doing. I had prayed about it and felt God was leading me in a different direction. My desire was to go to law school. Bev could have said, 'Are you crazy? Do you want to give up all this on a whim? What about the kids? Our friends? We've got everything. Why do you want to disrupt our home?' But you know, she didn't. She said, 'Ted, if that's what you want to do, then let's do it. We came into this marriage without a penny to our name. We know how to live frugally. Your happiness is more important to me that any material possession we have acquired. Let's go for it.'"

I talked to Beverly to get her perspective on what happened during that transitional time in their lives. "Bev," I asked, "what was going through your mind when Ted told you he wanted to go back to school?"

"While Ted was talking, I kept thinking about my own father," Bev explained. "He was unhappy in his job his entire life. I didn't want that for Ted. No amount of money is worth that. I understood that Ted would not be able to work while in school, at least for the first year. It was going to be very different from the lifestyle we were living, but I almost saw it as an adventure."

So off they went. We watched as Ted and Bev packed up their belongings and set out to make Ted's dream come true. Three years later, they moved back to town. Ted with a law degree and Beverly with two more babies.

"What if it hadn't worked out so well," I asked Ted. "How would you be feeling today?"

"Life is a risk," he answered. "We never know if the decisions we make will be successful. It could have gone very badly. One thing that was always evident with Beverly was that we were in this together. It started out as *my* dream, but it became *our* dream. If I succeeded, she succeeded. If I failed, she failed. I guess that has been the key to the success of our marriage in general."

"Was it hard?" I asked.

"Let's just say," Ted said with a raised eyebrow and slight laugh in his voice, "God was very present."

When it comes to our husbands, we have a choice. We can be their chief critic or their chief cheerleader. Oh sure, some days it flips back and forth from one to the other, but as for me, I want to follow Bev's lead and have those pom-poms ready to cheer my man on to victory.

Now, let's turn our attention to two different women who married men with one similar dream.

Two Tales of Two Writers
Wife Number One

When author and speaker Florence Littauer was a senior in college, she went home for Christmas vacation to watch her parents' store so that her mother and father could take their first vacation in years. The day before her parents were to leave for Boston, her father took her quietly aside to the little den behind the store. The room was so small that it held only a piano and a hide-a-bed couch. In fact, when you pulled the bed out, it filled the room and you could sit on the foot of it and play the piano.

The two of them walked into the back room and her father reached behind the old upright and pulled out a cigar box. He opened the lid and showed her a little pile of newspaper articles. I'll let Florence tell you what she discovered that day...

> "What are they?" I asked.
>
> Father replied seriously, "These are articles I've written and some letters to the editor that have been published."
>
> As I began to read, I saw at the bottom of each neatly clipped article the name Walter Chapman, Esq.
>
> "Why didn't you tell me you'd done this?" I asked.

"Because I didn't want your mother to know. She has always told me that since I didn't have much education, I shouldn't try to write. I wanted to run for political office also, but she told me I shouldn't try. I guess she was afraid she'd be embarrassed if I lost. I just wanted to try for the fun of it. I figured I could write without her knowing it, and so I did. When each item would be printed, I'd cut it out and hide it in this box. I knew someday I'd show the box to someone, and it's you."

He watched me as I read over a few of the articles and when I looked up, his big blue eyes were moist. "I guess I tried for something too big this last time," he added.

"Did you write something else?"

"Yes, I sent some suggestions in to our denominational magazine on how the national nominating committee could be selected more fairly. It's been three months since I sent it in. I guess I tried for something too big."

This was such a new side to my fun-loving father that I didn't quite know what to say, so I tried "Maybe it'll still come."

"Maybe, but don't hold your breath." Father gave me a little smile and a wink, and then he closed the cigar box and tucked it into the space behind the piano.

The next day, when Florence's parents left for the train station in Boston, her 73-year-old father fell over dead from a heart attack. Her mother returned home, relayed the story, and never shed a tear.

Florence concludes her story:

On the morning of the funeral, I sat at the table in the store opening sympathy cards and pasting them in a scrapbook when I noticed the church magazine in the pile. Normally I would never have opened what I viewed as a dull religious publication, but just maybe that sacred article might be there—and it was. *For More Democracy* by Walter Chapman.[1]

What would Walter Chapman have accomplished in his 73 years had his wife encouraged him to fulfill his dream rather than discouraging him from trying? We will never know. Now let's look at another man who dreamed of becoming a writer.

Wife Number Two

Nathaniel was a hardworking man who worked diligently in a customhouse in England many years ago. He was heartbroken as he walked home, thinking how he was going to tell his wife he had been fired from his job. However, when he delivered the news, he was quite surprised at her response.

"Now," she said triumphantly as she clapped her hands in delight, "you can write your book!"

"Yes," replied the man, with sagging confidence, "and what shall we live on while I am writing it?"

To his amazement, she opened a drawer and pulled out a substantial amount of money.

"Where on earth did you get that?" he exclaimed.

"I have always known you were a man of genius," she told him. "I knew that someday you would write a masterpiece. So every week, out of the money you gave me for housekeeping, I saved a little bit. Here is enough to last us for one whole year."

From her trust, confidence, and encouraging words came one of the greatest novels of American literature. That was the year Nathaniel Hawthorne wrote *The Scarlet Letter*.

Two men married to two very different wives. I imagine not many husbands aspire to become writers, but they do aspire to accomplish something in this world. They long to leave their footprint, to make a difference, to leave their mark. "Why is it that so few of us ever fulfill our potential? Is it because somewhere along the line someone whose opinion we valued gave us a discouraging word?"[2] The woman of your man's dreams is one who will encourage him in this great race of life. She will inspire him to reach for the stars, follow his dreams, and be all that God intends for him to be.

Deep inside every man is a little boy with great dreams to make a lasting impact on the world around him. There's a fireman who dreams of rescuing a damsel from the angry flames of a burning building, a pro basketball player who dreams of making the winning basket in double overtime, the warrior who dreams of destroying the evil foe and saving the world from destruction. We chuckle, but these are the imaginings of little boys and big boys alike.

When did the dream die? I suspect it never did. If you want to become the woman of your man's dreams, encourage him to dream again! Better yet, help him make those dreams a reality. Dream together. Plan together. Make a mark on your generation together.

Oliver Wendell Holmes once said, "Many of us die with the music still in us." May we speak positive words and learn how to open the music box to our husband's hearts to allow the melody to flow.

> *The woman of my dreams would dream about the future with me. I know my wife is busy taking care of the kids and working hard just to get everybody's needs met, but I wish she would dream with me more and be more affirming of my dreams and ambitions, rather than saying, "That's nice, honey." She doesn't say that all the time, but a little more excitement and dreaming would be nice.* —Frank

> *The woman of my dreams believes in me and my prospects. —Al*

> *My wife does a great job of encouraging me as the spiritual leader of our family. She looks past my faults. —Larry*

The Governor

Once there was a woman riding along in a limousine with her husband the governor. As they passed a group of men doing road construction, they noticed one of the workers was a man the wife had dated in high school. The governor smugly said, "Just think, honey, if you had married that man, you'd be married to a ditch digger."

The wife thought about that for a moment and then replied, "I don't think so, dear. If I'd married that man, he'd be the governor."

As women, we have the ability to encourage our men to accomplish great feats, or discourage them from reaching for their dreams. Oswald Chambers wrote: "Love is not blind; love sees a great deal more than the actual. Love sees the ideas, the potential in us."[3]

> *I wish my wife understood how it makes me feel when she puts me down in public or how it would make me feel if she would praise me in public. —Peter*

> *I wish my wife understood how important it is for me to feel needed and valuable. —Derek*

> *A woman can make or break a man. Mountains can be conquered when a man has a woman standing*

by him and supporting him. You have heard the saying "Behind every good man is a great woman." Nothing could be truer. You need only to look through history books at the great men of our time. A supportive and encouraging woman, one who builds a man up, will be first choice of a man every time.
—Jason

Twenty-Five Things to Never Say to Your Spouse

1. I told you so.
2. You're just like your father.
3. You never help me around the house.
4. You never listen to me.
5. You're always in a bad mood.
6. You're always _____.
7. You never _____.
8. You just don't think.
9. It's all your fault.
10. You should have listened to me.
11. What's wrong with you?
12. I wish you were more like _____.
13. All you ever do is complain.
14. I can never please you.
15. What did you expect?
16. You got what you deserve.
17. You're lazy.
18. If you'd have more ambition, you'd get somewhere in life.
19. You're irresponsible.
20. You're impossible.
21. What were you thinking?
22. I don't know why I put up with you.
23. I don't know how much more of this I can take.

24. God help you, I sure can't.
25. I can talk to you until I'm blue in the face and it doesn't do any good.

Twenty-Five Things Your Husband Longs to Hear

1. I'm so proud of you.
2. If I had to do it all over again, I'd marry you.
3. I missed you today.
4. I've been thinking about you all day.
5. I'm so lucky to have married a man like you.
6. What can I do for you today?
7. How can I pray for you today?
8. You are so strong.
9. Thank you for working so hard for our family.
10. Other men could learn a lot about _____ from you.
11. The best part of my day is when you come home.
12. You are one of God's most precious gifts to me.
13. Great job!
14. Thank you.
15. I'm sorry.
16. You are wonderful.
17. That was really great.
18. You're so smart.
19. You look so handsome in that shirt.
20. You make my day bright.
21. Thank you for being my husband.
22. I don't feel complete without you.
23. I appreciate all you've done for me this week.
24. I'm so glad I married you.
25. You are my best friend.

Section Seven

Sexually Fulfills Him

The First Chapter in His Book

Okay, ladies. While this may be the last section in *this* book, you can be sure it was the first chapter in his. From the surveys I collected, sexual fulfillment was right at the top of their list—no surprise! As a matter-or-fact, it was first and foremost, running neck and neck with respect. Sexual fulfillment is climactic in a man's life—no pun intended. If you excel in praying for him, respecting him, adoring him, initiating intimate friendship with him, safeguarding your marriage, and encouraging him, but neglect sexually fulfilling him, all your efforts will be for naught. Sexual fulfillment is the glue that holds all the other elements together. It is not just the glue of marriage. It is superglue.

Dr. Kevin Leman has counseled thousands of couples and has determined that a couple's sex life is a microcosm of the marriage. If the sex life is good, then the marriage is good. Very rarely does he see a bad marriage with a good sex life.[1]

When I began writing this book, I explained the project to several women's groups and encouraged them to have their husbands complete a survey.

"Ladies, I'm writing a book on how to become the woman of our man's dreams," I explained. "I know what you're thinking," I continued as I read the expression on their faces. "I don't need a book about that. I already know. Sex. Sex. Sex."

Well, I hope you've seen that becoming the wife of his dreams involves more than sex. However, if we already understand that sex is paramount, why aren't we more willing to make his dreams come true? Let's ponder that for a moment.

If your husband is sexually fulfilled, he will race a train, take a bullet, and climb the highest mountain to make sure you are okay. He will be a better father, better provider, better employee, and even a better sportsman. That's right. *Sports Illustrated* reported that behind every MVP is a good woman—and just one. Happily married men make better baseball players![2] (By the way, how did I know this? I entered into his world and read an article in *Sports Illustrated*.) All this because you have decided that you are going to be the wife of his dreams and make it your top priority to see that your man is sexually fulfilled.

This is what Dr. Kevin Leman has to say about the sexually fulfilled husband.

> A sexually fulfilled husband will do anything for you. Sex is such a basic need for men that when this area of their life is well taken care of, they feel immense appreciation and act accordingly. A sexually fulfilled man is the kind who drives to work thinking, *I'm so glad I married that woman. I must be the happiest man alive!* And who then drives home thinking, *What special thing can I do for my wife this evening?* If you want this kind of loyalty and appreciation, meet your husband's sexual needs; no other need generates such deep thankfulness. Instead of resenting requests to stop by the store or take a look at a leaky faucet, a sexually fulfilled man will jump with eagerness. Instead of being cold and distant when you talk to him, he's going to want to hear what you have to say.[3]

A man who is sexually fulfilled by the wife of his dreams will feel great about himself. He may not be king of the hill at the office, but if he knows he is the king of the hill in the bedroom, he'll keep a smile on his face and a skip in his step.

> *Women often trivialize men's sexual needs. I know too many men in dangerous situations because of this.* —Steven

> *I wish my wife understood my desire is to make sex last longer with more foreplay. Our greatest struggle has been the quality of our sex life.* —Will

> *On a scale of 1 to 10, sexual fulfillment for me rates at 11.* —Chris

> *What is the one thing I wish the woman of my dreams understood about me? Sex.* —Gene

> *Our greatest struggle has been physical intimacy. I believe that we need to work together, perhaps even through counseling, to move forward together on this.* —Andy

Divine Design

Have you ever stopped to think about the magnetism between a male and a female? Where did that come from? Why is it so strong? God put it there. Isn't He ingenious?

My maternal grandmother had 12 children and 10 miscarriages. (Count them. Yes, that is 22 pregnancies.) She was a farm girl who stayed pregnant most of her fertile life and died at the young age of 56. No wonder. My paternal grandmother was also a farm girl. She only had 6 children. Much to her mortification, I asked her how she prevented having children during the early 1900s. Her reply?

"I just didn't do the evil thing."

Oh my. "The evil thing," as Grandma Edwards called it, was created by God to be anything but evil. Proverbs 5:18-19 says: "May you rejoice in the wife of your youth. A loving doe, a graceful deer—may her breasts satisfy you always, may you ever be captivated by her love." Sex was God's idea! God took great care to make sexual relations between a husband and wife pleasurable, desirable, and fulfilling. It is a sinful world that has taken God's holy design and perverted, exploited, and sullied it.

We've visited the Garden of Eden a few times already, but let's take one more glimpse of our Creator and how He fashioned man and woman in His image. I don't want to embarrass, but encourage you to imagine God creating your husband, just as if he were the first man—Adam.

Going back to Genesis chapter 2, we read, "The LORD God formed the man from the dust of the ground and breathed into his nostrils the breath of life, and the man became a living being" (Genesis 2:7). "The LORD God said, 'It is not good for the man to be alone. I will make a helper suitable for him...So the LORD God caused the man to fall into a deep sleep; and while he was sleeping, he took one of the man's ribs and closed up the place with flesh. Then the LORD God made a woman from the rib he had taken out of the man" (Genesis 2:18,21-22).

Now, stop the cameras on this scene and let's use our imaginations for a moment. When we think of creation, we tend to think of the big picture: land and water, sun and moon, creeping animals and swarming seas. But I want us to turn our attention to the intricacies of the human body, features that were made, not just by the hand of God, but by the fingertips of God. The eyes, hair follicles, sweat glands, salivary glands, capillaries, eyebrows, cilia lining the nose, wrinkles of skin on the knuckles, toenails, and bumps on the tongue.

Let's envision God having a show-and-tell for the angels just before He woke Adam and Eve from their deep sleep. As the angels circled around the sleeping pair, God stood over His works of art to point out some of their unique features...

"Each aspect of these creations has a unique function crafted for a specific purpose," God explained. "Let's start at the top and work our way down."

God then explained how the hard skull served to encase the much softer brain just below the surface, and pointed out the specific function of each of the 206 bones of the body. He showed the angels how fingerlike nerve endings sent signals to the brain, how the heart pumped blood through veins, arteries, and capillaries like an ocean feeding rivers, streams, and tributaries, and how food would be taken into the mouth, flow down the esophagus, to the stomach and then filtered through the small and large intestines. For hours God excitedly pointed out one intriguing intricate detail after another. Finally, God reached just below the male and female waists where the organs for sexual reproduction are housed. "You'll find this very interesting," He said with great enthusiasm.

He first turned their attention to the male and showed the angels the tiny tubes where life-giving semen is created, stored, and released. "Every 48 hours or so, semen will build up and scream to be released. When properly stimulated by the woman, blood will fill the man's penis, causing it to become hard and erect. When the stimulation is continued, the semen, filled with microscopic sperm, will shoot forth with the force of a geyser and enter the woman. If one of the sperm reaches an egg and breaks through the protective covering, they will join just as the man and woman are joined and a new life will begin."

"How does the stimulation occur?" asked an angel.

"This fleshy tissue that you see lying here just between the man's legs is extremely sensitive to the touch. I have concentrated 17 sexual glands in this one area. The most sensitive part is the underside of the shaft and the head. The ridge on the bottom of the head and the indentation you see here on that ridge is hypersensitive."

"But God," the angels asked, "it is so flexible. How will it ever have the strength to enter into the female?"

"The penis may not look like much to you right now, but when the man's wife touches him, it is quite a different story."

"Amazing," they all agreed.

"But what about the woman?" one of the angels inquired. "She is very different."

"Yes," the Lord said. "She is created as the receptor for the man."

Then God explained how He worked with His fingertips to create the glove-type opening for the man's penis. He demonstrated how He scooped out an area that would receive the man and then went about meticulously creating other fascinating features.

God pointed out the ovaries where the eggs are created and the fallopian tubes where the eggs travel down to the uterus. He showed them the vagina and its placement just behind the urethra.

"You'll notice this fleshy knob of tissue just above the opening of the vagina. There are actually two sets, and outer and an inner set of fleshy lips. These are called labia. The outer labia are covered with hair, but the inner labia are not. Then right here is an extra sensitive area called the clitoris. It's hard to see, but it's at the hood of the inner labia. When the man stimulates this area, the woman will feel intense pleasure."

"It's so small," an angel mused. "How will the husband ever find it?"

"It may take some practice. But if he's smart, he'll search until he does. It's kind of like a treasure hunt! Just like with the male, when the clitoris is stimulated, it becomes larger and easier to find. It will actually protrude just a bit from hiding in the folds of the labia. What you see here is only the tip of the iceberg. The clitoris is about nine inches long and is nestled inside the woman's body, making the entire area sensitive to touch. However, when her husband touches her in the hypersensitive area, that iceberg will begin to melt and she will experience waves of ecstasy that will run through her entire body. The clitoris, like the penis, is very sensitive to touch and is the center of exquisite pleasure when handled properly or intense pain when handled improperly.

"Also, there's another secret spot just inside the woman's vagina opening on the front wall. When that is stimulated by the man, she will experience extreme arousal and eventual waves of ecstasy."

"But God, it seems that You have put a lot of detail and attention into the sensory component of the reproduction process for humans. I don't recall that for the other animals You have created," one of the angels noted.

"You are quite right," God responded. "I have gone to great lengths to create the intricate parts of both male and female reproductive organs. The sexual act for a male and female is not simply for reproduction. There are many sensitive areas I have fashioned for one purpose only—pleasure. This is my gift to them. Pleasure is not necessary for reproduction. I created them thus because I love them."

After God finished pointing out the other incredible intricacies of both the man and the woman, He breathed a strong wind over their bodies and stirred them awake.

Up to this point, we have no recorded words from the man Adam, but after he laid eyes on the fair Eve, he said, "Whoa, now this is good!" That's not exactly what he said, but that's what he meant. He said, "This is now bone of my bones and flesh of my flesh; she shall be called 'woman,' for she was taken out of man" (Genesis 2:23).

Are you blushing? I think it may be worth it. What I want you to realize is that sexual pleasure was created by a loving God. He formed you and your husband to give pleasure to and receive pleasure from one another. There are many facets of the human body that serve no other purpose. Science has shown us that all you need to make a baby is an egg and one tiny determined sperm. However, to make love, you need a lot more.

"The divine design is no mistake," writes author Gladys Hunt. "The mutual attraction of male and female calls us to confront our aloneness, out of our independence to see that we need each other. It is the foundation of human history. We are meant to enhance each other, to affirm each other's personhood and to discover that in our mutual dependence we solve the mystery of our existence."[4]

There may be a few of you who have tired of me continually going back to the Genesis account of how God created the universe and all it contains. Perhaps you have an evolutionary view of how the world began. But I daresay, if I ever had a doubt that there was a divine Creator, the sexual union between a woman and a man dismissed that doubt quickly. There is no way that could have "just happened"!

Author Stephen Schwambach writes:

> Anybody who has ever experienced great love-making instinctively knows the truth: Sex is too good to have just happened. It didn't evolve as the result of some cosmic accident. Something this exquisite had to have been lovingly, brilliantly, creatively designed.
>
> If an atheist ever comes up to you and demands proof that there is a God, all you have to answer is one word: "Sex." Give him a day to think about it. If at the end of that day he remains unconvinced, then he has just revealed far more about his sex life—or lack thereof—than he ever intended!
>
> God created sex. Doesn't that tell you a lot about who God really is? Among other things, it tells you that He is ingenious."[5]

I wish my wife would initiate sexual intimacy more often. I've read the books where I should start the whole day to get her thinking about it and looking forward to it, but it sure would be nice if she was the one who initiated it. —Brent

What is one thing I wish my wife understood better about me and what I long for? The need for her to be more sexual. I wish she'd be more creative and enthusiastic about it. I wish sex would be more fun and more of a priority in our marriage. —Rod

The woman of my dreams would want sex as much as I do. I don't think women really have a concept of how "wired" for sex men are. It can't make sense to them, not exactly sure why myself. It seems petty, but it's real. Also, the woman of my dreams would be confident in who she is, love the Lord deeply, and challenge me. —Aaron

TWENTY-SEVEN

Recharging His Battery

"I work hard all day," Jim explains. "When I come home, my greatest desire is to be recharged so I can go back out and do it all again the next day. What I wish my wife understood is that sex recharges me. She acts like it is a drain, but I wish she understood that when I'm left unfulfilled, it's like going to work with an empty tank."

Women tend to view sex very differently than men do. For us, sex does indeed begin in the morning with a kiss on the cheek, continues with a phone call in the middle of the day, and builds with help with the dishes after dinner. For a man, sex begins the moment his switch is flipped when you crawl into bed at night.

What recharges your battery? Shopping? Coffee with friends? Rest? Time alone? A pedicure? A spiritual retreat?

Guess what recharges your man's battery. Sex. If your husband is under stress because a project is due next week, one of the best gifts you can give him is to recharge his battery by making love and giving him the confidence he needs. Did his boss chew him out today? Did he lose that big order? Did he miss a deadline? Did he have to confront a coworker? There are many events in a man's day that drain his emotional battery. Sex with the woman of his dreams is God's unique physical and mental therapy prescription.

Dr. John Gray explained it this way: "Many times after having great sex with my wife, I realize that I had forgotten how beautiful the trees are in our neighborhood. I go outside and breathe in the fresh air and feel alive again. It is not that I didn't feel alive in my work, but by connecting with my wife through great sex, I can reawaken and bring my more sensual feelings that are easily forgotten in the focused pursuit of achieving my goals at work. In a sense, great sex helps me stop and smell the flowers."[1]

Sex is one of the most effective ways we can encourage and minister to our husbands. Through making love, we assure him that he is still desirable and very much a man.

Responding to Him

Do you want to know what your man desires more than anything? This may surprise you, but he wants to see *you* sexually fulfilled. He longs to see you respond to him. He wants to know that he is the one who can take you to the moon and back with a crescendo or ecstasy that *he* created. He longs to know that you are sexually aroused at his touch and that he is a great lover. When he sees you have an earthshaking orgasm, he thinks to himself, *I did that to her, thank you very much*. As Dr. Kevin Leman states, "There is not a man on the planet who doesn't want to know he can make his woman go crazy in bed."[2] "Even more than your husband wants to have sex with you for his own sexual relief, the truth is, he wants to please you even more than he wants to be pleased. It might seem like it's all about him, but what he really wants, emotionally, is to see how much you enjoy the pleasure he can give you. If he fails to do that, for any reason, he'll end up feeling inadequate, lonely, and unfulfilled. Most men want to be their wives' heroes."[3]

A husband is looking for fulfillment, not accommodation. Simply put, a husband is sexually fulfilled when his wife is fulfilled.

If he knows that she is not enjoying sex, but only trying to placate him, he will not be fulfilled. Sex may happen, he may finish what was begun, but he will have unfinished business in his heart. He will feel like a consumer, not a lover.

I want you and your husband to try an experiment. Find a piano bench and sit side by side before the ivory keys. Once you get comfortable, place both your hands on the keys and play a melodious duet, complete with highs and lows, rises and falls, sharps and flats.

What? You say that is ridiculous? You don't know how to play the piano? Well, why not? You have fingers. The piano has keys. It should come naturally, shouldn't it?

Very few people are born with the natural ability to play a piano by ear. The vast majority have to study the art and spend hours of practice before they can run their fingers over the keys to produce a beautiful melody. Some learn enough just to play "Chopsticks" and others progress to Beethoven's Fifth.

Likewise, for most people great sex does not come naturally. It takes practice and maybe even a little study. There are several great books on sex from a Christian perspective. Three of my favorites are *Intimate Issues* by Linda Dillow and Lorraine Pintus, *Sheet Music* by Dr. Kevin Leman, and *Intended for Pleasure* by Dr. Ed Wheat.

What about pornography? I suggest you stay as far away from pornography as possible. Videos and magazines have cheapened and sullied what God created as a beautiful expression of love between a husband and wife. The easy access of pornography through the Internet is a cancer ruining marriages all around the world.

Your husband has a dream to be *the* great lover and you are the chosen one to make that dream come true. In order to make that dream a reality, you may need to help him know what to do to bring you to a climax. Take his hands and move them to a place or places that please you. When something feels good, let him know. You'll not only be doing yourself a favor, you'll be doing him a favor as well.

Making love is much more than having sex. The purpose of the physical union is to love and be loved, to create a sense of oneness, to give yourself totally to your man. The goal is not to achieve orgasm. However, if a woman does not reach a climax a majority of the time she enters into sexual relations with her husband, she will be left feeling tense, frustrated, and dissatisfied.

It is a myth that orgasm should come naturally for a woman or that it is the man's total responsibility. Reaching a climax takes some effort on the wife's part as well. Very few women get a view from the top of the mountain without taking the effort to make the climb.

Here are a few interesting facts to keep in mind. A man usually needs about two to three minutes of stimulation to have an orgasm. A woman needs about ten times that amount.[4] A man's climax generally lasts from 10 to 13 seconds. A woman's lasts from 6 to 60 seconds.[5] The Latin word for clitoris means "little key."[6] For the majority of women, stimulation of the clitoris is the key to experiencing orgasm.

Going back to our piano scenario, all the keys are there to make beautiful music. The wife may simply need to help her husband know how to play the instrument.

> *I wish my wife understood my need to make time for intimacy a priority. Otherwise, she is a perfect wife!* —Allen

> *The woman of my dreams is one who is interested in sexually pleasing her husband by finding out what turns him on and exploring their sexuality together.* —Eric

> *Our greatest struggle has been our sex life. I guess it has been more of my struggle than hers. For so long*

I was reluctant to talk about it because I felt I was being selfish. But that struggle has led to temptations, to the point where I actually went to her and told her that I was having thoughts I shouldn't have. She was not angry but willing to change. However, change has not been easy. Her innocence was rooted in some feelings that sex was dirty—something wives had to do, not necessarily something they could enjoy. I think time is beginning to make things better, and I hope that our daughter will enjoy the same innocence but will take a different perspective about sex into her marriage. —Will

Give-and-Take

Sexual intimacy is a give-and-take process. A woman who fulfills her wifely duties out of obligation does not produce a sexually fulfilled husband. That would be like a husband handing his wife a dozen roses on their anniversary and saying, "I didn't really want to get you these roses. Seems like a waste of good money to me. But I read somewhere that I'm supposed to do something like this because it's our anniversary. Hope you enjoy them."

Would you enjoy such a presentation?

Let me share one of the secret desires that the survey respondents mentioned. Men dream of having their wives initiate sex more often. They want you to take, take, take. Notice I said "more often." Some of you are trying to remember if you've ever initiated sex, so imagine the joy on his face when you try it the first time.

"But what will he think of me? Will he think I'm a wanton, sex-crazed woman?" He might hope that's what you are, but he won't think that. He might be utterly confused at your sudden desire, but one message will come across loud and clear: "She wants me! She wants me!" You know what he'll feel. He will feel as though his dreams have come true.

I'm not suggesting that a man wants his wife to initiate sex all the time. That isn't the natural order of things. God created man to be the aggressor and woman to be the recipient. Even our sex organs are crafted this way. Men are hunters and women are gatherers. But I can promise you that every man likes to feel hunted and captured by the woman of his dreams. When it comes to give-and-take, your husband fantasizes that you would do a little taking.

> *Our greatest struggle has been in the area of sexual communication and understanding the difference in the importance it is for us individually and as a couple. We have had to learn to make time, to be vulnerable, and to seek each other's needs before our own. We have had to learn each other's "love language" and make adjustments to help meet the other's expectations and needs. The hardest problem is for my wife to understand that my desire for sexual expression is to give and express myself to her.* —Bill

> *I wish my wife would be more responsive to my sexual advances and more aggressive in her own advances.* —Dave

> *Women must understand that men show love by making love. Sexual fulfillment is not a dirty activity done out of duty.* —Craig

TWENTY-EIGHT

The Right and Fright
of Refusal

In the book of Proverbs, King Solomon tells his son the joys of having sexual relations with the same woman for his entire life. "Drink water from your own cistern, and running water from your own well. Should your fountains be dispersed abroad, streams of water in the street? Let them be only your own and not for strangers with you. Let your fountain be blessed, and rejoice with the wife of your youth. As a loving deer and a graceful doe, let her breasts satisfy you at all times, and always be enraptured with her love" (Proverbs 5:15-19 NKJV). That's great advice, but if the man goes to the well and the well is dry, he might be tempted to dip his cup elsewhere to quench his thirst.

Let's go back to Dr. Leman's quote on page 228. If you make it your mission to have a husband who is sexually fulfilled, "instead of resenting requests to stop by the store or take a look at a leaky faucet, a sexually fulfilled man will jump with eagerness. Instead of being cold and distant when you talk to him, he's going to want to hear what you have to say."

Dr. Leman goes on to say,

> Some wives reading this may be thinking, *I tried that, and it didn't work.* Such a response shows me

that you're misunderstanding me entirely. You can't just "try" this; it has to become a way of life. One good time of sex will make a man thankful—for a while. But if he's turned down the next five times he approaches you, he'll think about the five rejections, not that one special night.

Because of a man's chemical makeup, sex feels like a need to most of us, and when a woman graciously and eagerly meets that need, we become very thankful. When a woman uses a man's need to manipulate him, a man becomes resentful. When a woman uses a man's need to punish him, he often becomes bitter."[1]

It all goes back to the reasons why we want to become the woman of his dreams. Is it to give or to get? Oh, believe me, when you give in this area of his life, you will indeed reap many wonderful benefits. However, if we are giving in this area only to get, he will be able to tell—and so will God. In the Bible, we are warned that wrong motives will leave us empty (James 4:3).

When a wife refuses her husband sexually, she shouldn't be surprised when he refuses her practically (fixing a leaky faucet or running to the store). When she withholds sex as a weapon for manipulation, it will boomerang and come right back to her—aimed directly at the heart.

Proverbs 13:12 tells us that "hope deferred makes the heart sick." We've all seen it. Your husband comes slinking into the bathroom as you're washing your face before bed. He has that sheepish grin that you know so well, slides his hand around your waist, and says, "You tired?"

"Yep, sure am," you quickly reply.

The next look you see in the mirror from that man standing behind you? That is hope deferred personified. If his advances are dashed enough times, hope deferred becomes hope destroyed.

Let's look at what the Bible has to say about our right to refusal, for both the husband and the wife:

> The husband should fulfill his marital duty to his wife, and likewise the wife to her husband. The wife's body does not belong to her alone but also to her husband. In the same way, the husband's body does not belong to him alone but also to his wife. Do not deprive each other except by mutual consent and for a time, so that you may devote yourselves to prayer. Then come together again so that Satan will not tempt you because of your lack of self-control (1 Corinthians 7:3-5).

If ever there was a politically incorrect statement, this is one of them: "The wife's body does not not belong to her alone..." The mantra of the pro-abortion movement has been *It's a woman's body and she has the right to do with it as she pleases.* But Paul is saying it is *not* our body to do with as we please. Saying "I do" at the altar means we are committing to say "I will" in the bedroom.

Proverbs 31:12 tells us that the wife of noble character does her husband "good, not harm, all the days of her life." When we deny our husbands sexually, we are, in a sense, leading them into temptation. Paul tells us right there in 1 Corinthians 7 that when we deny our man, we are tempting him to look elsewhere. We are opening the door to Satan, and he is all too ready to pounce right in and devour.

I don't know about you, but that thought brings terror to my heart. That is the fright of refusal. Could I actually be tempting my husband to sin by denying him sexually? Yes. If we are not meeting our husband's needs, we are asking for trouble. This type of action, or I should say, lack of action, on our part will cloud his thinking, discourage his manhood, and encourage him to look elsewhere.

By our willingness to fulfill our husbands sexually, we can make him feel like the luckiest man on earth. On the other hand, by our constant rejection of his advances, we can make him feel defeated and deflated. We have a choice as to how we will make him feel: elated or emasculated, blessed or cursed, top dog or underdog. God has given us a lot of power! He must have thought we could handle it. How are you doing in this area?

We've already established that sexual fulfillment is a need in a man, not simply a want. Would you withhold food from a starving child if it was in your power to feed him? Of course not. And yet, when we withhold physical relations from our husbands, the results are somewhat the same.

Paul wrote to the Corinthians that husbands and wives have a "duty" to fulfill each other sexually (1 Corinthians 7:3). The word "duty" implies that sexual fulfillment is an unpleasant task that a spouse must perform whether he or she wants to or not. However, in the original Greek, "duty" is more of paying a debt that is owed. It is not an unpleasant task but a privilege.

When some people tithe, they see it as a burden that must be fulfilled, while others see it as an opportunity to give back to God. Paul said, "God loves a cheerful giver" (2 Corinthians 9:7). Sex is a wonderful opportunity for us to give back and, ladies, our men also love a cheerful giver.

A woman must never use sex as a weapon to punish her husband or as a reward to get what she wants. A prostitute sells sex for favors, not a wife. Along these same lines, a man who feels that he is begging or asking his wife for a favor is a man who feels humiliated rather than fulfilled. Ladies, sexual fulfillment for a man is more than ejaculation. Boy, that was hard to write, but some of us need to be shocked into understanding the truth.

The Bible tells us that "the wise woman builds her house, but with her own hands the foolish one tears hers down" (Proverbs 14:1). I think we need to be using our hands to build up our houses and build up our husbands, if you get my drift.

I hear women complain that their husbands won't talk to them. They desire to have a fluent line of communication running at all times. However, when a woman refuses her husband sexually, it is as if she is snipping the lines of communication one refusal at a time. Pretty soon, all lines are dead. No dial tone. Nada.

That doesn't mean it has to stay that way. A little electrical work and you're back in business. However, if the lines have been out for quite some time, it may take time to make the connection work properly again. You may even get a few wires crossed, but don't give up.

I'm not saying that a wife must say yes to sex every time her hunk of burning love approaches her, but she does need to be careful how she responds. If I learned anything from the hundreds of men who answered my survey, I learned men are very fragile when it comes to their sexuality. Compare these two scenarios:

Scenario Number One

Clyde comes slinking into the bathroom as Betty is putting the finishing touches on her 15-minute face cleansing and moisturizing regiment. He runs his hand down her back and grins.

"Not now, Clyde," Betty snaps. "I've had a hard day and that's the last thing on my mind."

Scenario Number Two

Frank comes slinking into the bathroom as Teresa is putting the finishing touches on her 15-minute face cleansing and moisturizing regiment. He runs his hand down her back and grins.

"Now that's a nice idea," she replies. "I'll tell you what, big guy. I had an extremely tiring day today, but if you'll hold that thought until tomorrow, I'll make it a night you won't soon forget."

I venture to say that both men will be disappointed, but only one will feel dejected. Ladies, if you do ask for a continuance, keep your promise and make it worth his wait. You better believe he'll be thinking about you all the next day and don't be surprised if he comes home early!

What if your husband is pressuring you to do something that you are not comfortable with? I suggest you tell him in a loving way that you are not comfortable with that suggestion. But, if it is something that is not wrong, just different, you might consider trying it out. A husband should never pressure his wife to perform sex that makes her feel degraded. Love does not "demand its own way" (1 Corinthians 13:5 NLT), especially in the bedroom.

> *I wish my wife understood that meeting my sexual needs is like putting money in the bank. Men long for passion in a relationship.* —Justin

> *My wife is very responsive to me sexually and emotionally. We enjoy our times of intimacy very much.* —Paul

> *One thing I wish my wife understood is that sexual contact makes me feel close to her, just like spending time and talking to her makes her feel close to me.* —Stan

The following is a prayer request that I received at Proverbs 31 Ministries:

My husband and I have been married for almost seven years now. The whole time I have had a problem with my sex drive. This led to him finding what he wanted on the Internet and he would also call other women and talk to them. When I found this out, he apologized and said he would never do it again....He has recently gotten a new secretary and she brings him hot chocolate in the morning and they spend all day together in the office. He also calls her on his cell phone very often. I have questioned him about this, and he thinks I am just too jealous and it is stupid for me to act this way. I just need help in letting the past be the past and trusting him…

You know where the first red flag popped up in my mind? "I have had a problem with my sex drive." Let's just stop right there. What have you done to correct the problem? I am not making excuses for men who go to chat rooms or porn sites. I am not making excuses for men who have affairs with their secretaries, either mentally or physically. However, this young gal needs to realize that when she is not meeting her husband's sexual needs, she is tempting him to get those needs met elsewhere. But when we have a husband who is sexually fulfilled, he'll be saying, "There's no place like home!"

TWENTY-NINE

Get Creative

When I mentioned how God created the intricacies of man and woman in the beginning of this section, I forgot to mention man's largest sexual organ—the brain. Hot-wired to the brain are his eyes, which run a direct circuit to his private parts below.

God created men as visual creatures. They like what they see and they see what they like. This is why men, in general, like to make love with some light on in the room. This is why a man, exhausted from an arduous day in the office or on the field, can catch a glimpse of his wife undressing and be ready and raring to go. This is why advertisers use beautiful women to sell cars, trucks, razors, and a passel of other products.

Create a Lovely Atmosphere

It is amazing what a simple candle can do. He wants to see you, and I don't know anyone who doesn't look better by candlelight than an overhead light. Consider creating a lovely atmosphere in your bedroom. Avoid making your sleeping quarters the catchall for the laundry, mail, or records. Consider making the bedroom the most beautiful room in the house with attractive furnishings, warm lighting, and cozy, welcoming bed linens.

Create a Lovely Wife

Sandra Aldrich was speaking at a women's retreat when a lovely young woman approached the podium. She took her offered hand and then whispered, "I really appreciate what you just said about the importance of the sexual side of marriage, but I've gained so much weight after our three boys that I don't like my husband to see me."

The confession surprised Sandra and she responded, "But you're beautiful." The woman stared at Sandra, wanting to believe her words. "I mean it," she assured her. "You are a lovely young woman. Sure, your body isn't a size eight, but it's produced three healthy little boys. Is your husband upset?"

The woman shook her head. "No, he acts as though I'm still the size I was when we married. The problem's mine." She gestured to her hips.

"Honey, stop putting yourself down," Sandra insisted. "You are beautiful, so don't let those few extra pounds put a barrier between you and your husband." Sandra lowered her voice to match the young woman's and gave her some woman-to-woman advice about what a husband wants. As she blushed, she gave her arm a little squeeze. "Tonight you just forget about the size of your thighs and love your husband the way he wants you to—and the way you want to. Make that man glad he babysat today so you could come to this retreat."[1]

I daresay, if this woman followed through, her husband will be busy signing his wife up for every women's retreat that comes along.

According to a *Psychology Today* survey, more than half of all American women dislike their overall appearance.[2] I've often heard that when a man looks in the mirror, he focuses on his best feature, but when a woman looks in the mirror, she focuses on her worst. I'm guilty as charged.

When it comes to sexually fulfilling our husbands, they are much less concerned with the extra pounds or the cellulite than we may think. Don't get me wrong. As we have already discovered, men do want an attractive spouse. However, inner confidence is incredibly irresistible to a man.

So let's look at a few ways to boost our confidence in the lovemaking department to accentuate the positive.

One way for a woman to prepare her mind and emotions for an enjoyable evening of lovemaking is to make herself beautiful. Take a bubble bath. Spray on a favorite cologne. Put on enticing lingerie.

Spend some time at a lingerie store and discover what brings out your best features.

"But he doesn't even let me keep the lingerie on for five minutes!" you may say. Believe me—more importantly, believe the men from my survey. It is a powerful five minutes. He loves it. It shows him that you have given your lovemaking some forethought. Besides, who doesn't like to unwrap a package!

Over the past several years, we've become lazy with our gift presentation. When I was a child, we painstakingly wrapped our presents with lovely paper and tied them with colorful bows. Today, we've moved to the gift-bag approach: Plop a present in a bag, stick in two sheets of tissue paper, and voilà. It looks pretty enough, but let's be honest. Do you get more excited pulling something out of a bag, or plucking off a bow, ripping through the paper, and tearing off the lid? I'm all for the wrapping myself.

Let's think about the gift we're giving our husband when we crawl into bed. Gift bag or beautifully wrapped present? The end result will be the same, but, oh, the fun and excitement he'd have peeling off the wrapping! Now don't get me wrong. Most men would just be satisfied with the gift bag approach. Proverbs 5:18 tells a husband to rejoice in the wife of his youth. I just think we should give him something to rejoice about.

Create a Relaxed Woman

Have you noticed that your husband is never too tired for lovemaking? Just as I have a special compartment for dessert, no matter how much I've had for dinner, Steve has a special compartment for lovemaking, no matter how tired he may be. When I'm tired, I'm tired. When Steve's tired, he's never too tired.

Men have an Energizer battery on reserve at all times. It automatically recharges every day—no matter what. If your husband had been working on a hot asphalt roof replacing shingles in 100-degree heat, took a shower, collapsed in exhaustion on the couch, and then was awakened by his scantily clothed wife with that special twinkle in her eye, he'd be raring to go. It is the eighth wonder of the world.

Let's face it. Being a woman is tiring. On any given day we are a housekeeper, interior decorator, laundress, gourmet chef, short-order cook, chauffeur, painter, wallpaper hanger, seamstress, nurse, guidance counselor, internal affairs CEO, financial planner, travel agent, administrative assistant, disciplinarian, preacher, teacher, tutor, spiritual advisor, dietician, lecturer, librarian, fashion coordinator, private investigator, cheerleader, manicurist, pedicurist, automobile maintenance expert, referee, and gift purchasing agent to both sides of the family. Now we're going to be the sex goddess in the bedroom? Calgon, take me away!

Actually, that might be a great place to start, in the bathtub. On those days when you know that a sexual interlude is probable, why not begin by taking a warm relaxing bath to help the tension knots dissolve with the soap bubbles? I think Calgon had the right idea.

Fatigue is a real problem for women. Here's what one women's magazine had to say:

> What's the first thing to go when you're busy, tired, and stressed? If you said sex, you're not alone. An estimated 24 million American women say they don't have time, are too exhausted, or just aren't in the mood for sex, and more than a third of Redbook readers say that being too tired is their number one excuse for not having sex. So we put it off for later—but later can easily become never. In

case you haven't noticed, abstinence doesn't make the loins grow hotter, it just begets more abstinence.

Sex, on the other hand, begets more sex. Studies show that lovemaking elevates the levels of brain chemicals associated with desire. So the best way to increase your yearning for sex is to have it.[3]

If you are too tired because you are too busy, I suggest attacking your Day-Timer or calendar with a good sturdy eraser. What are you doing that someone else could do? What are you doing that is taking valuable time away from your family that needs to be eliminated from your schedule? If you are out of the house more than two nights a week, then you're gone too much. Go to a mirror and practice saying the word no. Saying no to a plethora of outside activities may give you just the energy you need to saying yes to your husband in the bedroom.

If necessary, mark specific days on your calendar for intimacy. This may sound too planned and predictable for some folks. After all, isn't making love supposed to be passionate and spontaneous? Sometimes it is and sometimes it isn't. I daresay your husband will be happy either way. We make regular appointments for checkups, haircuts, aerobic classes, and lunch dates with friends. Doesn't it make sense to make working to improve or maintain a strong marriage part of your busy schedule?

Create a Healthy Woman

God intends for a woman to enjoy intimate sexual experiences with her husband. There's no other explanation for that small organ just above the opening of the vagina. He put it there for your pleasure. So if you are having difficulty in this area, you shouldn't be embarrassed or ashamed to seek medical, psychological, or even spiritual intervention.

The American Psychiatric Association lists four categories of female sexual disorders: sexual desire disorder, sexual arousal disorder, orgasmic disorder, and sexual pain disorder. If any of these symptoms occur on a consistent basis, a woman needs to seek medical intervention.

Besides physiological problems, a woman may experience psychological problems that come into play. Depression, guilt, stress, past sexual abuse, and premarital sex are just a few conditions that can inhibit an enjoyable sexual experience. Studies show that 25 percent of all females are sexually abused before they reach adulthood.[4] If your past is impeding your present, seek help. Don't suffer needlessly or wait until your husband walks out in frustration.

Men and women are taking more medication than at any time in history. It seems there is a drugstore on every corner in my hometown. People respond differently to various medications and sexual side effects are common.

Dr. Judith Reichman wrote:

> Many drugs have both a direct effect on our brain and central nervous system and a local effect on our genitalia, and on occasion that drug's action on one may contradict its effect on the other. For example, an antidepressant might boost our mood and make us more likely to want sex, yet if it increases serotonin levels in the brain we wind up with lowered libido. Birth control pills might correct certain hormonal imbalances but may also diminish testosterone levels and libido. On a more local basis, some women find birth control pills increase vaginal lubrication while others find the opposite to be true, especially if they develop more yeast infections and pain with intercourse.[5]

If you are taking a medication of any kind and suspect it may be affecting your sex drive or ability to reach a climax, talk to your doctor. The remedy may be as simple as changing your dosage or switching to a different drug.

Create Anticipation

Men operate like a light switch—either off or on. However, women are more like a dimmer switch. We start with just a hint of light and then the beam grows as the switch is adjusted. It takes a man just a few seconds to prepare for sex, but it can take a woman several hours to warm up to the idea.

So what's the solution if your husband doesn't understand that sex begins with a hug in the morning and help around the house in the evening? Perhaps we need to start the Crock-Pots ourselves. Begin the day by thinking about the evening and planning accordingly.

You know what I've discovered? I simply told my husband that when he helps me out around the house, it makes me want to please him. We're not exchanging favors. I'm not paying him for being "a good boy." It's just fact. When I feel he is loving me by unloading the dishwasher and putting away folded laundry (these have become two of his favorite pastimes), it makes me want to eat him up with a spoon! He's figured this out and whistles as he carries the laundry basket up the stairs in the evening.

Stephen Covey, author of *The Seven Habits of Highly Successful People*, says that all things are created twice, first mentally and then physically. The key to creativity is to begin with the end in view, with a vision and a blueprint of the desired result.[6] By creating a visual image of making love with your husband, you will be building anticipation in your own mind and be several steps closer to the desired result.

In Linda Dillow and Lorraine Pintus' book *Intimate Issues*, they tell a story about a woman named Heidi. She asked her husband, Brent, what he would like for his birthday present. She expected him to say something ordinary, like new golf clubs. Instead, his extraordinary request stunned her: "Honey, the only gift I desire is for you to give yourself permission to be a sensuous woman." Heidi's eyes filled with tears.[7]

One thing that was so precious to me as I read the responses from the men who completed my survey is that they love their wives. The woman of their dreams is a combination of deeply spiritual and divinely sexual. Those two compartments are not separate. They are one and the same, and I've come to realize that men have a better handle on that than most of us ladies.

Sexual fulfillment between a husband and a wife is not only the dream of your man, it is the design of a holy God.

> *The woman of my dreams is sold-out for God. She is a spiritual and sexual person—a prayer partner and a sexual partner.* —Kevin

> *My wife is the woman of my dreams. I know that she loves and respects me. Our greatest struggle has been our sex life. I wish she understood that I need to be needed in a physical way. I don't want her to view the physical aspect of our life as a chore or an obligation that she has as a wife, but something she looks forward to as a woman. Her innocence as a teenager and young woman attracted me, but as the years go by, I guess I long to see her grow into a woman who is not embarrassed by her needs.* —Al

> *In a world where there is so much temptation facing men, I think it's important for wives to know when to stop being "wife and mom" and start being a "lover."* —Buck

Twenty-Five Tips for Making Sparks Fly

1. Make the master bedroom the most beautiful room in the house. Why do we give so much attention to the living room where nobody goes and so little attention to the master bedroom where we spend almost 33 percent of

our married lives? Avoid making it the catchall for unfolded laundry or paper clutter. The bedroom is for rest and romance. Let's make sure to create an environment that invites both.

2. Invest in some yummy scented candles for the bedroom. We've already established that most of us look better by candlelight, so let's make it enticing to the sense of smell as well.

3. Play some soft music to set the mood.

4. Make lingerie part of your clothing budget. Sexy lingerie doesn't have to be expensive, and this is one area where your husband won't mind you spending a few extra dollars—I promise. And remember…when it comes to lingerie, less is more.

5. Take a bubble bath to relax before a romantic evening. If there's room, make it a bubble bath for two.

6. Reserve one special perfume that you wear only for those intimate nights together. The scent alone will be all the encouragement he needs. You might even want to dab a bit in some unusual places and see if he can find where the scent is coming from.

7. Rent a hotel room occasionally. It's not cheap, but it costs less than a divorce. This is especially enticing if you still have children in the home. A "one-night stand" in a hotel room makes a wonderful birthday or anniversary present. You might have a difficult time explaining what you gave him to his friends, but the grin on his face would give it away regardless.

8. Silence is not golden when it comes to lovemaking. Let him know what pleases you, that he's driving you crazy, that he's turning you into an animal. That's a song he'll play in his heart over and over again. If you feel uncomfortable, begin small, but begin.

9. Say your husband's name during lovemaking. "I love you, _____."

10. Make love in a different room in the house.

11. Get creative. You would never serve your husband the same meal every night. Think of various ways to serve up his favorite dish—you!

12. Ask your husband what you could do to bring him pleasure.

13. Tell your husband what you find irresistible about his body.

14. Write him love notes or "invitations" on the bathroom mirror with soap.

15. When he's in the shower, hide all his underwear.

16. Surprise him by joining him in the shower.

17. Put a towel in the dryer for a few minutes and then wrap him in it when he gets out of the shower.

18. Turn off the television and turn on your husband instead.

19. Cut up all your flannel nightgowns and use them for dusting cloths.

20. Give your husband the gift of a fast and furious "quickie." While the dimmer switch approach may be more appealing to you, a quick flash of lightning may bring out the beast in your man. Let him growl!

21. Make a rose petal path from the back door (or whatever door he enters from work) to the bedroom. Have the kids visiting a friend for the evening.

22. Place a special "invitation" in his briefcase before he goes to work or in his suitcase before he leaves on a trip. Let him know you'll be anxiously awaiting his return.

23. Undress slowly.

24. Undress him slowly.

25. Invest in satin sheets.

What Will the Future Hold?

Bruce and Mary Ellen grew up in the mountains of North Carolina in the sleepy little hollow of Waynesville. From Bruce's first remembrance, he recalls the petite beauty with chestnut hair, Coke-bottle figure, and "plenty of book smarts." Back in the 1940s, high school only went through eleventh grade, with an optional twelfth for those who wanted to continue in their studies. Since Mary Ellen was one grade behind, Bruce made the decision to stay one more year…to continue his studies, of course. Bruce and Mary Ellen were a stunning couple. His muscular build with 32″ waist and 6′4″ stature towered over Mary Ellen's 5′3″ with curves in all the right places. No one was surprised when Bruce asked Mary Ellen to be his bride just a few days after her graduation. On a beautiful November afternoon in 1943, they became husband and wife. When they said those words, "till death do us part," they meant it. It was a vow made to one another and to God, and the thought of anything other than a lifelong commitment to each other was inconceivable…no matter what.

It was war time when Bruce and Mary Ellen tied the knot, and 11 months after they were married, Bruce was shipped off to the

Aleutian Islands. For the next 18 months, the newlyweds corresponded through the U.S. mail. There were no telephones, e-mails, or instant messaging. The communication of two hearts depended on prayer, pen, and paper. In one of his many letters, Bruce asked Mary Ellen to send him a photograph of her legs... which she did.

Never was a man so happy as when Bruce got off the bus, walked to Mary Ellen's grandparents' house, and saw his bride come bounding down the steps in her nightgown to rush into his hungry arms. Never again were they apart for an extended period of time.

Bruce went right to work when he arrived back in the United States, but he had a dream to go to college. Three years later, even though they now had a two-year-old baby girl in tow, Mary Ellen encouraged him to follow his dream. Bruce graduated from college with a master's in education and then for the next 39 years served as a teacher, a coach, a high school assistant principal, and a junior high principal. Through the years, Mary Ellen had various jobs, but she retired after being with one company for 25 years. Together they raised four wonderful children...and one of them became my husband on a beautiful summer day in August of 1980.

In November of 2003, we celebrated Bruce and Mary Ellen Jaynes' sixtieth wedding anniversary. I was in the throes of writing and was hit with the realization of the living example of what I hope this book will help others accomplish. Mary Ellen was and is the woman of her man's dreams—and she has been for 60 years. Faces lined with years embrace cheek to cheek, weathered hands and arthritic fingers intertwine, and slow but steady gaits serve as a picture of enduring love in the winter of their lives. Like a rare treasure, their legacy of commitment and enduring love is the inheritance they leave to four grown children and five grown grandchildren. Oh, and that picture of her legs that Mary Ellen mailed Bruce in 1944 when he was off at war? He still carries that photo in his wallet today.

Imagine with me for a moment. Think ahead 20, 40, 60 years. What do you see? Your marriage is becoming what it is going to be—and so much depends on you. No, building a wonderful marriage cannot be achieved by one party alone. It takes two. I take that back. It takes three: A woman who's committed to becoming the woman of her man's dreams; God, who longs to give her the power and creativity to do so; and a man who clings tightly to both.

I pray that you and your husband's lives will be so intertwined that you will not be able to see where one ends and the other begins, and that your hearts will beat in tandem with each other to the metronome of God's pulse. And then one day, as your husband reflects on the years you've invested, he will say, "Many women do noble things, but you, my dear, surpass them all."

Praying Scriptural Prayers for Your Husband from Head to Toe

Sometimes we simply don't know how to pray for our husbands. However, when we pray the Word of God, we can be sure we are praying the will of God. God calls us to cover the saints with our prayers, so what better way to pray for our husbands than starting at the head and covering him down to his toes? The following is a list of verses that I've combined to pray the Scripture for our husbands. Just begin by inserting his name in the prayers.

His Head

Lord, as my husband is the head of our household, I pray he will look to You as the head of his life (Ephesians 5:23; 1 Corinthians 11:3). Help him to take the leadership role in our home and seek Your wisdom in every decision he makes, knowing that the fear of the Lord is the beginning of wisdom (Psalm 111:10).

Help him to know that the very hairs of his head are numbered and You care for each detail of his life (Luke 12:7).

His Mind

Lord, I pray for my husband's mind. I know that You do not give a spirit of fear, but of love, power, and a sound mind (2 Timothy 1:7 KJV). Make him of sound mind today and take away any confusion. May he have the mind of Christ and think as the Holy Spirit would lead him and not the flesh (1 Corinthians 2:16).

I pray he will not be conformed to this world but transformed by the renewing of his mind with Your Word day by day (Romans 12:2). Because every spiritual battle of temptation is won or lost at the threshold of the mind, I pray that my husband will turn from temptation as soon as the thought enters his mind (James 4:7). I pray that he will recognize the temptation, reject the temptation, and rejoice that he had the strength to refuse the temptation (1 Timothy 6:11; 2 Timothy 2:22; 1 Corinthians 6:18). Just as God warned Cain that "sin is crouching at your door," I pray that my husband will recognize when sin is crouching at the door, and master it—beginning with his thoughts (Genesis 4:7). I pray he will be able to take every thought captive to the obedience of Christ (2 Corinthians 10:5).

As You promised that You will keep in perfect peace those whose minds are steadfast, secured, and stayed on You, I pray my husband will experience that peace today as his mind is fixed on You (Isaiah 26:3). Finally, whatever is true, whatever is noble, whatever is right, whatever is pure, whatever is lovely, whatever is admirable—if anything is excellent or praiseworthy—may he think about such things today (Philippians 4:8).

His Eyes

Lord, Jesus taught us to pray, "Lead us not into temptation" (Matthew 6:13). I pray that You will steer my husband's eyes away from temptation today. From the Internet to magazines, from billboards to women he meets in the workplace, keep his eyes from lingering on images that will be harmful to his thought life. Help him to take the way of escape by clicking "delete," removing himself from the situation, or focusing his eyes on a different image (Mark 9:47). Keep him from committing adultery in his heart by looking at other women (Matthew 5:28).

Open his eyes to see Your greatness in creation and to see that Your mercies are new every morning (Lamentations 3:23). Help him to see trials as learning opportunities (James 1:2-3), to see Your fingerprints on each day of his life, to see Your provision and protection. May he be confident in this, that he will see "the goodness of the LORD" (Psalm 27:13). Open his eyes that he may see wonderful things in Your Word (Psalm 119:18). May his eyes be open when You are doing a new thing in his life and opening up ways in the desert or streams in the wasteland (Isaiah 43:19).

Just as You asked the blind men, "What do you want me to do for you?" and they answered, "Lord, we want our sight," I pray the same for my husband (Matthew 20:32). Help him to see You today. Your Word says that those who look to You have faces that are radiant and never covered with shame (Psalm 34:5). May his eyes look to You today. May he look to You for strength (Psalm 105:4). As the eye is the lamp of the body, may his eyes be filled with good things today (Luke 11:34).

His Ears

Just as I pray for You to lead my husband away from temptation by what he sees with his eyes, I pray You will lead him away from temptation with what he hears with his ears.

May he hear Your still small voice today (1 Kings 19:12 NKJV) and listen as You instruct him (Deuteronomy 4:36; Psalm 32:8). I pray he will listen to You and not turn away (Isaiah 50:5). I pray he will hear You telling him when to turn to the left and to the right, that he will listen to wise counsel from his friends and coworkers (Proverbs 1:5) and stay away from those who talk as fools (Proverbs 10:21). I pray he will walk away from coarse jesting, filthy talk, and off-color jokes (Ephesians 5:4).

His Mouth

Lord, I pray the words of my husband's mouth will be pleasing in Your sight today (Psalm 19:14). I pray no unwholesome word would come from his mouth, but only what is helpful for building others up according to their needs, that it may benefit those who listen (Ephesians 4:29). Set a guard over his mouth and keep watch over the door of his lips (Psalm 141:3). Put words in his mouth so that he may make Jesus known to those around him (Ephesians 6:19).

Lord, I pray You will keep him from coarse jesting and inappropriate language (Ephesians 5:4). I pray he will be a man of honor and keep his word to his family, friends, and coworkers (Matthew 5:37). I pray he will do everything without complaining or arguing so that he may become blameless and pure (Philippians 2:14-15).

Help him not be hasty in his speech (Proverbs 29:20) but slow to speak and quick to listen (James 1:19). Whatever he says today, may he be a good representative for You (Colossians 3:17).

His Neck

Lord, in the Old Testament, those who refused to obey You were called stiff-necked, so today I pray my husband will be submissive to You (Nehemiah 9:29). Your Word promises that obedience to Your law results in a long and peaceful life (Proverbs 3:1-2). Jesus said, "If you love me, you will obey what I command" (John 14:15). I pray my husband will demonstrate that love for You today by obeying Your commands.

I pray he will be strong, courageous, and careful to do everything written in Your Word so that he will be prosperous and successful today (Joshua 1:8-9). Help him to see that Your precepts are good (Psalm 119:128-129). I pray he will believe in the name of Jesus Christ and love others as You have commanded us to do (1 John 3:23). I pray he will humble himself before You today so that You will lift him up (James 4:10). May he have the mind of Christ, who although was God Himself, humbled Himself by taking the form of a man and obeyed even to the point of dying on the cross (Philippians 2:6-8).

His Arms

Lord, many times Your strength is personified by Your outstretched arm (Exodus 15:16; Deuteronomy 7:19; 11:2). Today I pray for my husband's arms and his strength—that he will clothe himself with Your strength (Isaiah 51:9). I pray my husband will see that he has You to help him fight his battles (2 Chronicles 32:8). May You be the strength of his life and his portion forever (Psalm 73:26).

Stand by his side and give him strength (2 Timothy 4:17). Help him to realize and call on the power of the Holy Spirit to give him the strength to do all that You have called him to do (Ephesians 1:19). Thank You that You have promised to give him strength to do all that You have called him to do if he would but ask (Philippians 4:13). I pray he will love You with all his heart and with all his soul and with all his mind and with all his strength (Mark 12:30).

I pray my husband will long to embrace me with his arms (Song of Songs 2:6). That his arms will long to embrace me and only me (Proverbs 5:20).

His Hands

Lord, today I pray for the work of my husband's hands. I pray he will enjoy the good of all his labor and see it as a gift from God (Ecclesiastes 3:13; 5:19). I pray he will neither be lazy (Proverbs 10:15) nor a workaholic (Proverbs 23:4-5), but have the right balance. May he have clean hands and a pure heart before You (Psalm 18:20).

May the favor of the Lord rest upon him and establish the work of his hands for him (Psalm 90:17). I pray he will mind his own business and work with his hands so that he may win the respect of outsiders and not be financially dependent on anybody (1 Thessalonians 4:11-12). I pray he will have success and know that his success is from You (1 Samuel 18:14).

I pray my husband may find Your purpose for him in what he does with his hands today. Help him to be faithful in the little things at work so that he will be entrusted with much more (Luke 16:10). When he comes up against a difficult situation, I pray he will turn to You and remember that God's grace is sufficient for him, for God's power is made perfect or visible when we depend on Him (2 Corinthians 12:9).

Whatever his hands do today, I pray he will work as working for the Lord and not for men since that is where his ultimate reward will come from (Colossians 3:23-24). At the end of the day, I pray he will not be ashamed to lift up holy hands in praise or fold his hands in prayer.

His Heart

Lord, I pray my husband will love You with all his heart (Deuteronomy 6:5) and trust You with his whole heart (Proverbs 3:5). Create in him a clean heart today (Psalm 51:10), and help him draw near to You with a sincere heart full of assurance of faith (Hebrews 10:22). May Your peace rule in his heart (Colossians 3:15). Above all, I pray he will guard his heart, for it is the wellspring of life (Proverbs 4:23).

Lord, I ask that my husband will be able to love his enemies and pray for those who persecute him (Matthew 5:44). I pray he will love his neighbors (Matthew 22:39) and his brothers in Christ (1 Peter 1:22). I pray Your love may abound still more and more in real knowledge and all discernment, so that he may approve the things that are excellent, in order to be sincere and blameless (Philippians 1:9-10 NASB). I pray he will be rooted and grounded in love, and that he will be able to comprehend the breadth and length and height and depth of Your love for him today (Ephesians 3:17 NASB).

I pray also that the eyes of his heart may be enlightened in order that he may know the hope to which God has called him, the riches of God's glorious inheritance in him, and God's incomparably great power for him who believes (Ephesians 1:18-19).

> *If your husband is not a Christian, his salvation is your most urgent prayer. Everything else pales in comparison. You've probably already discovered that believing in Jesus Christ is not something you can "talk him into." Only God can quicken his heart to believe.*

Lord, I pray my husband will come to know you as his Savior and Lord. I pray he will understand that while he was yet a sinner, You demonstrated Your own love for him and sent Your Son to die on the cross to pay the penalty for his sins (Romans 5:8). I pray he will one day confess with his mouth that Jesus is Lord, and believe in his heart that You raised Him from the dead

(Romans 10:9). I pray he will call on the name of the Lord and be saved (Romans 10:13).

His Side

Lord, I pray for those with whom my husband walks side by side. I pray for his friendships. I pray that he will have godly friends who will sharpen him as iron sharpens iron (Proverbs 7:17), who will hold him accountable to live a godly life (Proverbs 28:23), and who will step in and help him bear burdens when they grow too heavy for him to bear on his own (Galatians 6:2). I pray he will have friends who will stand with him for what is right and good, and pick him up when he falls (Ecclesiastes 4:10).

I pray my husband will choose his friends wisely (Proverbs 12:26) and avoid forming friendships with men who will lead him down a wrong path (1 Corinthians 5:13). I pray he will be a good friend and consider ways to encourage those who walk with him (Hebrews 10:24-25).

His Body in General

Lord, I pray my husband will be in good health today (3 John 1:2). I pray he will see his body as the temple of the Holy Spirit and take care of himself (1 Corinthians 3:16). I pray You will make his bones healthy so that he will be like a well-watered garden and like a spring of water that does not run dry (Isaiah 58:11). I pray he will fear the Lord and shun evil as to bring health to his body and strength to his bones (Proverbs 3:7-8).

His Legs

Lord, I pray my husband will stand firm in the teachings of Christ today (2 Thessalonians 2:15). I pray he will be strong in the Lord and in His mighty power by putting on the full armor of God so that he will be able to stand against the devil's schemes

(Ephesians 6:10-11). Increase his faith, for by faith we are able to stand firm (2 Corinthians 1:24). Your Word says that You give "strength to the weary and increase power of the weak. Even youths grow tired and weary, and young men stumble and fall; but those who hope in the LORD will renew their strength. They will soar on wings like eagles; they will run and not grow weary, they will walk and not faint" (Isaiah 40:29-31). That is my prayer for my husband today.

His Feet

Lord, I pray you will order my husband's steps today, so that his eyes will look straight ahead and fix his gaze directly on You (Proverbs 4:25). I pray he will walk in the way You have commanded (Deuteronomy 5:33). I pray Your love will ever be before him as he walks in Your truth (Psalm 26:3).

Blessed is the man who walks not in the counsel of the ungodly (Psalm 1:1 NKJV) but fears the Lord and walks in His ways (Psalm 128:1). I pray tht my husband will walk with wise men so that he also may be wise (Proverbs 13:20). I pray he will run the race with endurance and not stumble along the way. I pray he will throw off any sin that entangles him and slows him down (Hebrews 12:1 NASB). I pray Your Word will be a lamp to my husband's feet today and a light to his path (Psalm 119:105).

I pray my husband will walk in truth, in light, and in tandem with Christ today (1 John 1:7). "For the LORD God is a sun and shield; the LORD bestows favor and honor; no good thing does he withhold from those whose walk is blameless. O LORD Almighty, blessed is the man who trusts in you" (Psalm 84:11-12).

Study Guide

Lesson One: Prays for Him

1. Read the following verses and note what you learn about consistency in prayer:

   a. 1 Thessalonians 1:2-3

   b. Romans 1:9-10

   c. Ephesians 6:18

   d. Colossians 1:3

   e. 2 Timothy 1:3

   f. After reading these verses, how often do you think you should pray for your husband?

2. How does Paul encourage us to pray in 1 Thessalonians 5:17-18?

3. Why can we give thanks in all circumstances according to Romans 8:28?

4. What does Matthew 18:19-20 tell us about the power of having a prayer partner?

5. Is there someone with whom you can pray for your husband, your marriage, and yourself? Have you ever considered praying with your husband as well as for your husband?

6. What do you learn about God's power from Romans 4:17? How does that encourage you today?

7. What does Psalm 5:3 tell you about David's certainty that God would answer his prayer?

8. Consider starting a prayer journal or journal page singularly for your marriage.

Lesson Two: Prays for Him

1. Sometimes when I don't know what to pray for someone, I turn to Paul's letters and use his prayers as a guide. Read the following prayers and note what Paul prayed for his friends:

   a. Ephesians 1:15-23

    b. Ephesians 3:14-19

    c. Philippians 1:9-11

    d. Colossians 1:9-14

2. What does the latter part of James 5:16 tell us about prayer?

3. Compare the following translations of James 5:16:

   "The prayer of a righteous man is powerful and effective" (NIV).

   "The effective prayer of a righteous man can accomplish much" (NASB).

   "The effectual fervent prayer of a righteous man availeth much" (KJV).

    a. Define "righteous."

    b. Who is righteous? (Romans 6:18)

    c. Define "effective."

    d. Define "fervent."

    e. Now go back and note any further insight you may have into what can be learned about prayer from James 5:16.

4. We can pray for someone and we can pray with someone. What does Paul urge his friends to do in Romans 15:30?

Paul writes, "join me in my struggle." The Greek word for "struggle" is *sunagonizomai*, which means "to struggle in the company of; to be a partner, strive together." How can we struggle with someone in prayer?

5. How do the following verses show two people on the same side of a struggle?

a. Galatians 6:2

b James 5:16

c. Romans 12:15

6. If you are willing to make a commitment to pray for your husband every day, fill in your names in the following:

I _____ (your name), commit to pray for my husband _____ (his name) every day. I commit to pray for his spiritual growth, for him to have divine wisdom, and for him to grow closer to Christ. I also commit to pray for myself, that I may be the wife my husband needs.

7. Pick one passage of Scripture from question number one and put your husband's name in the prayer.

Lesson Three: Respects Him

1. Read these verses and note any fresh insight into the roles of husbands and wives:

   a. 1 Corinthians 11:3

   b. Ephesians 5:22-33

   c. Colossians 3:18-21

   d. 1 Peter 3:1-7

2. During the reign of King David, he brought the once-captured ark of God back to Israel. It was one of the grandest moments in his life. Read the account recorded in 2 Samuel 6.

   a. How did David's wife, Michal, react to David's outward praise of God? (6:16,20)

   b. What was David's response to her? (6:21)

   c. What was the outcome of her disrespect? (6:23)

3. We don't know much about Noah's wife, but we do know she must have been a very patient woman!

   a. In what condition do we find the world in Genesis 6:5-7?

   b. What did God tell Noah to do (Genesis 6:13-22) and why did He pick Noah? (Genesis 6:8)

   c. What was Noah's response? (Genesis 7:5)

   d. Many Bible scholars believe that there had never been rain on the earth before this time. Rather, a mist covered the earth much like a greenhouse effect. If that was the case, how does obedience to build a boat seem even more radical?

e. It took a very long time to build the ark. Most assuredly there were many onlookers who taunted and hurled insults at Noah and his family. Let's just suppose Noah's wife had tired of being looked down upon, not submitted to her husband's leadership, and refused his request. What would have happened to her in the end?

4. Make a list of any ways that you have not been respecting your husband. What are you willing to change? Be specific.

Lesson Four: Respects Him

1. We've looked at what submission is, so now let's turn our attention to what submission is not. Submission does not mean following a husband into a sinful situation. Read Acts 5:1-11. How did Sapphira follow her husband's lead? What was the result?

2. Submission to our husband's leadership does not mean that we have no opinion or do not voice our concerns. Note the reason that Pilate was hesitant to condemn Jesus to death recorded in Matthew 27:19.

3. Submission does not mean that a woman has no initiative or drive. Look up the following verses from Proverbs

31 and note the woman of noble character's business savvy:

    a. Proverbs 31:14

    b. Proverbs 31:16

    c. Proverbs 31:18

    d. Proverbs 31:24

4. From what you have learned in the second section of *Becoming the Woman of His Dreams* and lessons three and four of the study guide, write a definition of biblical submission in marriage.

5. As mentioned in chapter 8, taking care of our outward appearance is a way of showing respect to our husbands. A happy or confident woman is a beautiful woman. Note what the following verses say about the source of beauty:

    a. Psalm 19:8

    b. Psalm 34:5

    c. Proverbs 15:13

    d. Isaiah 61:1-3

    e. 1 Peter 3:3-5 (Note the word "merely" in the NASB.)

6. Read the following account of Mary and Martha in Luke 10:38-42. Using your imagination, what do you think Mary looked like? What do you think Martha looked

like? Who do you imagine was more beautiful? Interestingly, we are never told about either woman's appearance, but I have always imagined Mary as beautiful. Could it be because she spent more time at Jesus' feet?

7. God has invited you to come to His spa each day—to sit at His feet and be transformed by His Word. Are you willing to accept this invitation?

Lesson Five: Adores Him

1. Read the following verses and note what they say about loving deeply:

   a. Matthew 18:21-22

   b. 1 Corinthians 13:4-8

   c. Ephesians 4:32

   d. 1 Thessalonians 4:9-10

   e. 1 John 4:11

2. Read Romans 12:9-21 and make a list of the various aspects of love. Now go back and put a check mark beside the ones you do well as a wife and a minus by the ones that need improvement.

3. Read and record Matthew 6:21. Do you think your husband feels that he is a treasure to you?

4. Answer the following questions and then review those answers with your husband. You might want him to answer them as well.

   a. The first time I saw you I thought...

   b. The thing that attracted me most about you was...

   c. The first time we kissed, I felt...

   d. The first time I dreamed about being married to you was...

   e. The best date we ever had before we were married was...

Lesson Six: Adores Him

1. What is one aspect of love mentioned in 1 Peter 4:8?

2. What do the following verses teach about forgiveness?

   a. Luke 11:4

   b. Luke 17:3-5

   c. Colossians 3:12-14

3. Read Matthew 9:1-8. Which did Jesus feel was more important—forgiveness or physical healing? What does that say to you?

4. Read Matthew 18:23-35. Which character do you resemble most in this parable?

5. How are we to forgive according to Ephesians 4:32 and Colossians 3:13? What does that look like to you?

6. How are we putting ourselves in danger when we choose not to forgive?

   a. 2 Corinthians 2:10-11

   b. James 5:16

7. Read Philippians 3:13. Part of forgiving is leaving the past behind and reaching forward to what lies ahead. Is there something in your marriage that you need to put behind you? Is God calling you to let go of a past hurt or offense and move forward?

Lesson Seven: Initiates Intimate Friendship with Him

1. We don't know much about Priscilla and Aquila, but we do know that this couple shared a common passion for spreading the gospel. Read the following verses and note what you learn about their partnership in ministry: Acts 18:2; 18:26.

2. The most intimate friendship occurs with the uniting of spirits. What did Jesus pray in John 17:20-23? Who is Jesus referring to in John 17:20? What are some ways you

can develop intimate friendship with your husband on a spiritual level?

3. One aspect of friendship is described by the words "one another." Read the following verses and note what you learn about "one anothering."

   a. Romans 12:10

   b. Galatians 5:13

   c. Ephesians 4:2

   d. Ephesians 4:32

   e. Ephesians 5:21

   f. 1 Thessalonians 5:11

   g. Hebrews 10:25

   h. James 4:11

   i. 1 Peter 3:8

   j. 1 Peter 4:9

   k. 1 Peter 5:5

   l. 1 John 4:7

3. From the above verses, which ways do you "one another" well and which ways could use some improvement?

Lesson Eight: Initiates Intimate Friendship with Him

1. Another word for "friend" is "companion."

   a. Define "companion."

   b. With that definition in mind, read and record Genesis 2:18.

   c. Other than procreation, what reasons would you give as to why it is not good for man to be alone?

2. What do the following verses tell us about friendship?

   a. Proverbs 18:24

   b. Ecclesiastes 4:9-10

   c. Song of Songs 5:16

   d. John 15:13

3. In Exodus 17 we see the story of Moses and the Israelites fighting against their enemies, the Amalekites. As long as Moses stood with the staff of God raised into the air, the Israelites were winning, but whenever he lowered his hand, the Amalekites prevailed (verse 11). What did Hur and Aaron do to help their friend Moses? (verse 12). How can the woman of your man's dreams help support him in order for him to have victory in the battles he faces every day?

4. In chapter 15, I mentioned Sheldon Vanauken's warning against "creeping separateness." Do you sense that any

areas of your marriage could be possible threats to draw you and your husband apart or cause you to move in opposite directions? If so, discuss them with your husband and consider making necessary changes.

Lesson Nine: Safeguards Her Marriage

1. Read and record Proverbs 4:23.

   a. In a dictionary, look up and define "wellspring."

   b. What insight can you glean from this definition?

   c. What happens when a wellspring is contaminated?

2. What do the following verses tell us about feelings we might have that tell us that we or our husbands are impervious to attack?

   a. Proverbs 16:18

   b. 1 Corinthians 10:12

   c. 1 John 1:8

3. The book of Proverbs is a compilation of life lessons that a father is teaching to his son. In the first chapters he focuses on the dangers of adultery and flirting with temptation. These lessons can apply to us women as well. The results are the same for both men and women who

break marriage vows. Read the following verses and note the end result of having an affair.

   a. Proverbs 5:1-6

   b. Proverbs 5:15-23

   c. Proverbs 7:10-27

4. Where is our best place of refuge according to Psalm 7:1?

5 What are we told to do when tempted by sexual immorality? (1 Corinthians 6:18)

6. In Song of Songs 2:15, the lover warns his beloved about the little foxes that sneak in and ruin the vineyard. Can you think of any little foxes that have snuck into your marriage bed?

Lesson Ten: Safeguards Her Marriage

1. In chapter 20, we looked at how King David did not safeguard his marriage; however, it takes two to tango. Let's go back and read 2 Samuel 11.

   a. Where was Bathsheba bathing? Was she discrete?

   b. How could she have prevented tempting her neighbor?

   c. Could she have refused David's invitation?

   d. What part did she play in this sordid affair?

2. What does Romans 14:21 teach about not causing someone to stumble? This verse is talking about eating various foods, but how could it apply to the way we dress or the way we act around other men?

3. Look up and define the word "flirt." List ways to avoid flirting with other men or curtail them from flirting with you. For example, when I'm on an airplane and a man gets a bit too friendly, I ask him about his wife and children and even ask to see their pictures.

4. Flirting with your husband can be fun! The Song of Songs is full of flirtatious words and actions between the beloved and the lover. What are some ways you can flirt with your husband? Example: Wink at him from across the room.

5. What does Paul tell us in 1 Thessalonians 5:22?

6. Abstaining from the appearance of evil is not just for appearance's sake. Most sinful behavior begins with the eyes and the mind. How have you seen this to be true? How can abstaining from the "appearance of evil" protect someone from actually doing something wrong?

7. What was Paul's struggle in Romans 7:15-18 and 22-24? What was the solution to his struggle? (Romans 7:25). Also note Philippians 4:13.

Lesson Eleven: Encourages Him

1. Read and record Hebrews 10:24.

   a. What ways can you encourage your husband today? This week? This year?

   b. "Let us consider how we may spur one another on..." (Hebrews 10:24). Define the word "consider." Does the word imply a quick glance or careful thought?

   c. Define the word "spur." The Greek word for "spur" means "to sharpen alongside." Look up and record Proverbs 27:17. How can you and your husband sharpen each other with encouraging words?

   d. Spur, the noun, can be painful. Spur, the verb, can motivate and encourage. Which are you?

2. What did Job's wife encourage him to do? (Job 2:9).

3. Read Judges 16.

   a. What did Delilah encourage Samson to do? (Judges 16:4-7,10-12,13-14).

   b. How did she manipulate him? (Judges 16:15-16)

   c. How did her words cause his demise? (Judges 16:17-19).

4. To contrast the devastating effects of negative words, the Bible tells of many women who encouraged the prophets. Read and note how the following women

encouraged various men to accomplish what God had called them to do.

   a. Judges 4:1-14

   b. Mark 15:40-41

   c. Luke 8:1-3

5. Can you think of some ways you can encourage your husband to accomplish a task he feels God has called him to do?

6. Philippians 4:8 is a guideline for our thoughts, but this verse also has excellent advice for the words we speak. List the filter through which our words should pass.

7. Read and record Proverbs 12:4. Who wears a crown? Think of some ways that you can make your husband feel like the king of his castle this week.

Lesson Twelve: Encourages Him

1. One of the most important ways we can encourage our husbands is by giving the gift of encouraging words. Read the following verses. Make two columns and note the results of encouraging words and the results of discouraging words.

   a. Proverbs 10:11

   b. Proverbs 10:20

c. Proverbs 12:18

d. Proverbs 15:1

Encouraging words	*Discouraging words*
a. a fountain of life	violence

2. What do the following verses tell us about the power of our words?

   a. Proverbs 11:9 (Remember: your husband is your closest neighbor!)

   b. Proverbs 16:28

   c. Proverbs 21:23

   d. Proverbs 25:15

   e. James 3:5-6

3. What do the following verses tell us about the importance of thinking before we speak? It may help to change the "he" to "she" and "man" to "woman."

   a. Proverbs 13:3

   b. Proverbs 17:27-28

   c. Proverbs 18:13

   d. James 1:19-20

4. Ephesians 4:29 is a good plumb line for the words we speak. Make a list of four guiding principles found in this verse.

1.

2.

3.

4.

5. What was David's prayer regarding his words? (Psalm 19:14; 141:3)

Lesson Thirteen: Sexually Fulfills Him

1. In the Song of Songs, the bride and groom talk about lovemaking in terms of a garden (Song of Songs 4:12,16; 5:1; 6:2).

   a. With that in mind, what picture does Proverbs 24:30-31 paint of a garden that is left unattended?

   b. Can you draw a parallel between the gardener in Proverbs 24:30-31 and the woman who neglects the garden of lovemaking with her husband?

   c. Walls were used to protect one's property from would-be bandits and enemies. The lazy farmer in Proverbs 24:30 has walls that have gone to ruin and crumbled. How could this relate to a marriage where the wife neglects the sexual fulfillment of her husband? How is she leaving him vulnerable to attacks?

d. Who is lying in wait for the unprotected and what does he desire to do? (John 10:10).

e. When Satan left Jesus after tempting Him in the desert, when does Scripture say he would attack again? (Luke 4:13).

f. What does that tell us about when and where the enemy attacks?

g. What does that tell us wives about making sure the "walls" around our husbands' sexual needs are fortified?

2. Read the following verses and note how the beloved (bride) looked forward to lovemaking. (Remember, the lover and the beloved compare lovemaking to a garden of delicious fruit!)

a. Song of Songs 1:2

b. Song of Songs 1:4

c. Song of Songs 2:3

d. Song of Songs 4:16

e. Song of Songs 7:11-13

3. Read Song of Songs 1:13 and note how the beloved enticed her lover.

4. Read the following verses and note how the beloved praised her lover's physical features.

    a. Song of Songs 1:16

    b. Song of Songs 2:3 (What is the difference between an apple tree and a cedar tree?)

    c. Songs of Songs 5:10-16

    d. How do you think your husband would feel if you made a list of features you love about his body and then read them to him before making love? Why not give it a try!

Lesson Fourteen: Sexually Fulfills Him

1. God has intended that marriage be an everlasting covenant between a man and a woman. Look up and define the word "covenant."

2. "Covenant," by definition, implies permanence. When God makes a covenant, how long does it last? (Genesis 9:16; 17:7; Jeremiah 50:5).

3. It has been said that "every divorce is the death of a small civilization." What does this statement mean to you?

4. Look up Genesis 2:24 and note what you learn about "leaving and cleaving" (KJV). The New International Version uses the words "be united to his wife." Look up and define the words "united" and "cleave." What insight do you gain?

5. A synonym for the word "united" is "amalgamated." Amalgamation is the process of melting down two or more metals and blending them together. Once the two

metals are joined, there is no way to separate them back out into their individual original forms. You can melt them down and mix other metals with them, but they cannot be purely separated again. How is this a picture of the amalgamation that happens when a man and a woman are united in marriage?

6. Read what the following verses say about divorce:

   a. Malachi 2:13-16

   b. Matthew 19:8

7. In Ephesians 5:25-32, Paul reminds husbands and wives that marriage is a living example of the relationship of Christ and His bride, the church. With that in mind, how does breaking the marriage covenant also break God's heart?

8. Would you be willing to renew your marriage vows to God and to your husband? If you can, go back and write out the vows you and your husband said on your wedding day. Type them out in a beautiful font or write them in calligraphy and consider placing them in a prominent place in your home.

9. If you are doing this Bible study in a group, share one thing from this book and the Bible study that you feel you do well. Share one area in which you need to improve and your plan for making those improvements.

Notes

Chapter 2
1. Donald Kaufman, S.M. Henriques, *God Can Handle It...Marriage* (Nashville: Brighton Books, 1998), p. 78.

Chapter 3
1. Kenneth L. Barker and John R. Kohlenberger III, *Zondervan NIV Commentary of Old Testament* (Grand Rapids, MI: Zondervan Publishing House, 1994), p. 8.
2. *Strong's Exhaustive Concordance* (Grand Rapids, MI: Baker Book House, 1987), p. 478.
3. W.E. Vine, Merrill F. Unger, William White Jr., *Vine's Complete Expository Dictionary of Old and New Testament Words* (Nashville: Thomas Nelson Publishers, 1985), p. 330.

Section 2
Chapter 5
1. Karol Ladd, *The Power of a Positive Wife* (West Monroe, LA: Howard Publishing Co., 2003), p. 100.

Chapter 6
1. Thomas H. Maugh II, "Marriage? It's Her Way or the Highway," *Los Angeles Times* (February 21, 1998).
2. Sheldon Vanauken, *Under the Mercy* (San Francisco: Ignatius Press, 1985), pp. 194-95.

Chapter 7
1. Kathy Bergen, "Richer but Not Happier," *Charlotte Observer* (September 10, 2000), p. D1.
2. Ibid.

3. Ibid.
4. Ibid.

Chapter 8

1. Willard Harley Jr., *His Needs, Her Needs* (Grand Rapids, MI: Fleming H. Revell, a division of Baker Book House Company, 1986), p. 10.
2. "Snapshots," as quoted in *Intimate Issues* by Linda Dillow and Lorraine Pintus (Colorado Springs, CO: Waterbrook Press, 2002), p. 58.
3. Nancy Wartik, *Glamour*, May 1996, p. 223, as quoted in *Intimate Issues*, p. 58.
4. Willard Harley, *His Needs, Her Needs*, p. 105.

Chapter 9

1. Taken from Ed Wheat, *Love Life for Every Married Couple* (Grand Rapids, MI: Zondervan, 1980), p. 177.

Section 3

Chapter 10

1. Bill and Anabel Gillham, *He Said, She Said* (Eugene, OR: Harvest House Publishers, 1995), p. 108.
2. Willard Harley Jr., *His Needs, Her Needs*, p. 151.
3. Ibid., p. 159.
4. Karol Ladd, *Power of a Positive Wife*, p. 36.
5. To learn more about the five love languages, see Gary Chapman, *The Five Love Languages* (Chicago, IL: Northfield Publishing, 1992, 2004). Used by permission.

Chapter 11

1. C.S. Lewis, *Mere Christianity* (Nashville: Broadman and Holman, 1996), p. 104.
2. Philip Yancey, *What's So Amazing About Grace?* (Grand Rapids, MI: Zondervan, 1997), p. 155.
3. Henry Blackaby and Richard Blackaby, *Experiencing God Day-by-Day* (Nashville: Broadman and Holman, 1997), p. 193.
4. Stormie Omartian, *The Power of a Praying Wife* (Eugene, OR: Harvest House Publishers, 1997), p. 13.
5. Spiros Zodhiates, et al., eds., *The Complete Word Study Dictionary: New Testament* (Chattanooga, TN: AMG Publishers, 1992), p. 229.
6. Karol Ladd, *The Power of a Positive Wife*, p. 60.
7. Lewis Smedes, *Forgive and Forget* (San Francisco: Harper and Row, 1984), pp. xxi, 146.
8. Alice Gray, Steve Stephens, John Van Diest, compilers, Lists to Live By for Every Married Couple (Sisters, OR: Multnomah, 2001), p. 170.
9. Anabel Gillham, *The Confident Woman* (Eugene, OR: Harvest House Publishers, 1993), pp. 145-146.

Chapter 12

1. Dennis Rainey, *Lonely Husbands, Lonely Wives* (Renamed *Staying Close*) (Dallas: Word, 1989), p. 31.
2. Connie Grigsby, "The High Calling of Being a Suitcase Remover," *P31 Woman*, January 2003, pp. 8-9.

3. Rick Warren, *The Purpose Driven Life* (Grand Rapids, MI: Zondervan, 2002), p.155.
4. Gary and Barbara Rosberg, *Divorce-Proof Your Marriage* (Wheaton, IL: Tyndale House Publishing, 2002), p. 116.
5. Alice Gray, et al., *Lists to Live By for Every Married Couple,* p. 28.

Chapter 13
1. Alan McGinnis, *The Romance Factor* (New York: Harpercollins, 1982).

Chapter 14
1. Linda J. Waite and Maggie Gallagher, *The Case for Marriage* (New York: Doubleday, 2000), p, 148.
2. Judith Wallerstein, Julia Lewis, and Sandra Blakeslee, *The Unexpected Legacy of Divorce* (New York: Hyperion, 2000), p. 295.

Section 4
Chapter 15
1. John M. Gottman and Nan Silver, *The Seven Principles of Making Marriage Work* (New York: Crown, 1999), p. 17.
2. Sheldon Vanauken, *A Severe Mercy* (New York: Bantam Books, 1977), p. 27.
3. William and Nancie Carmichael, compilers, quoting Sheldon Vanauken, quoted in *601 Quotes About Marriage and Family* (Wheaton, IL: Tyndale, 1998), p. 80.

Chapter 16
1. Willard Harley Jr., *His Needs, Her Needs,* p. 10.
2. Leil Lowndes, *How to Make Anyone Fall in Love with You* (Columbus, OH: McGraw Hill, 1996), p. 106.
3. Adapted from Willard Harley Jr., *His Needs, Her Needs,* pp. 79-80.
4. Al Janssen, *The Marriage Masterpiece* (Colorado Springs, CO: Focus on the Family, 2001), p. 84.

Chapter 17
1. James Dobson, *Solid Answers* (Wheaton, IL: Tyndale, 1997), p. 398.
2. Mark Price, "Get a Life," *Charlotte Observer* (November 1, 1998).
3. Dennis Rainey, *Staying Close* (Dallas: Word, 1989), p. 216.
4. Charles Swindoll, *The Grace Awakening* (Dallas: Word, 1990), pp. 5-6.
5. Gary and Barbara Rosberg, *Divorce-Proof Your Marriage,* p. 212.

Section 5
Chapter 18
1. Sandra P. Aldrich, *Men Read Newspapers, Not Minds* (Wheaton, IL: Tyndale House Publishers), p. 145.
2. James Dobson, *Solid Answers* , p. 480.
3. Sandra P. Aldrich, *Men Read Newspapers, Not Minds,* p. 140.

Chapter 19
1. Rob Parsons, "Don't Let Your Baby Drive You Apart," *Focus on the Family,* February 1998, p.12.
2. Ibid.

Notes

3. John Roseman, "Promise Keepers Challenges Husbands, but What About Wives?" *Charlotte Observer,* February 10, 1998, p. E6.

4. Ibid.

5. Mary Brenin, quoted by Carol Wallace, "Seven Ways to Find Romance When You Have Little Kids," *Redbook,* July 1998, p. 96.

6. Jay Belsky and John Kelly, "The Transition to Parenthood," quoted in Wallace, "Seven Ways to Find Romance When You Have Little Kids," *Redbook,* July 1998, p. 96.

Chapter 20

1. Lolly Winston, "Why You Can Love Your Husband and Brad Pitt Too," Family Circle, June 10, 2003, p. 40.

2. Ibid. p. 42.

3. William E. Vine, *Vine's Expository Dictionary of Old and New Testament Words* p. 297.

Chapter 21

1. <www.dhs.gov/dhspublic/display?content=157>.

2. William E. Vine, *Vine's Expository Dictionary of Old and New Testament Words,* p. 282.

Section 6
Chapter 22

1. William Barclay, *The Letter to the Hebrews, The Daily Study Bible* (Edinburgh: St. Andrews Press, 1955), pp. 137-38.

Chapter 23

1. Pam Kelley, "Can This Marriage Be Saved," *Charlotte Observer,* February 11, 2001, p. E1.

2. Al Janssen, *The Marriage Masterpiece,* p. 44.

3. Bill and Anabel Gillham, *He Said, She Said,* p. 129.

4. J. David Branon, "Sharing the Load," *Our Daily Bread,* June, 1992, no. 3.

Chapter 24

1. Anabel Gillham, *The Confident Woman,* pp. 216-17.

2. Florence Littauer, *The Gift of Encouraging Words* (Dallas: Word Publishing, 1995), p. 2.

3. Sharon Jaynes and Lysa TerKeurst, *A Woman's Secret to a Balanced Life* (Eugene, OR: Harvest House Publishers, 2004), p. 61.

4. Florence Littauer, *Silver Boxes* (Dallas: Word Publishing, 1989), p. 4.

Chapter 25

1. Florence Littauer, *Silver Boxes,* pp. 125-127. Used by permission.

2. Ibid., p. 129.

3. Alice Gray, et al., *Lists to Live By for Every Married Couple,* p. 28.

Notes

Section 7

Chapter 26

1. Kevin Leman, *Sheet Music: Uncovering the Secrets of Sexual Intimacy in Marriage* (Wheaton, IL: Tyndale House Publishers, 2003), p. 10.
2. Hank Ersch and Kostya Kennedy, "Scorecard," *Sports Illustrated,* August 17, 1998.
3. Kevin Leman, *Sheet Music,* p. 46.
4. Gladys Hunt, *Ms Means Myself* (Grand Rapids, MI: Zondervan, 1972), p. 28.
5. Stephen and Judith Schwambach, *For Lovers Only* (Eugene, OR: Harvest House, 1990), p. 127.

Chapter 27

1. John Gray, *Mars and Venus in the Bedroom* (New York: HarperCollins, 1995) p. 63.
2. Kevin Leman, *Sheet Music,* p. 52.
3. Ibid., p.11.
4. Linda Dillow and Lorraine Pintus, *Intimate Issues,* p. 39.
5. Carolyn Hagan, "How to Make a Good 'O' Great," *Glamour,* May 1998, p. 287.
6. Linda Dillow and Lorraine Pintus, *Intimate Issues,* p. 196.

Chapter 28

1. Kevin Leman, *Sheet Music,* p. 47.

Chapter 29

1. Sandra Aldrich, "Seven Ways to Put the Sizzle Back into Your Marriage," *Today's Christian Woman,* September/October 1997, p. 82.
2. Cited in Nancy Stedman, "Love Your Body," *Redbook,* May 2001, p. 46.
3. Susan Crain Bakos, "The Sex Trick Busy Couples Swear By," *Redbook,* March 2001, p. 125.
4. Kevin Leman, *Sheet Music,* p. 208.
5. Judith Reichman, *I'm Not in the Mood* (New York: William Morrow and Company, 1998), pp. 61-62.
6. Stephen Covey, *The Seven Habits of Highly Successful People* (New York: Simon and Schuster, 1989), pp. 98-99.
7. Linda Dillow and Lorraine Pintus, *Intimate Issues,* p. 13.

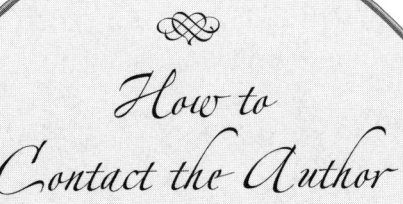

How to Contact the Author

Sharon Jaynes is an international inspirational speaker and Bible teacher for women's conferences and events. She is also the author of several books, including *Becoming the Woman of His Dreams, Becoming a Woman Who Listens to God, Ultimate Makeover,* and *Dreams of a Woman: God's Plans for Fulfilling Your Dreams.* Her books have been translated into several foreign languages and impacted women all around the globe. Sharon and her husband, Steve, live in North Carolina, and have one grown son, Steven.

Sharon is always honored to hear from her readers. Please write to her directly at

Sharon@sharonjaynes.com
or at her mailing address:

Sharon Jaynes
P.O. Box 725
Matthews, North Carolina 28106

To learn more about Sharon's books and speaking ministry or to inquire about having Sharon speak at your next event, visit

www.sharonjaynes.com.

Other Good Harvest House Reading

A Wife After God's Own Heart
By Elizabeth George
One secret to marital bliss is for a wife to love her husband the way God designed for her to love him. The rewards for doing so are rich! *A Wife After God's Own Heart* examines 12 key insights for a more fulfilling marriage.

The Power of a Praying® Wife
By Stormie Omartian
Bestselling author Stormie Omartian shares how wives can develop a deeper relationship with their husbands by praying for them. In this timeless book packed with practical advice on praying for specific areas, including decision making, fears, spiritual strength, and sexuality, women will discover the fulfilling marriage God intended.

Romancing Your Husband
By Debra White Smith
Wives, revolutionize your marriage! This unique book challenges women to cut through traditional misconceptions and explore the total Bible message on marriage. Author Debra White Smith covers everything from lifting up husbands in prayer to arranging romantic interludes.